S0-CBL-324

Proofs of Christianity

Charles Harris

GOSPEL PUBLISHING HOUSE
SPRINGFIELD, MISSOURI
02-0911

© 1977 by the Gospel Publishing House
Springfield, Missouri   65802
Adapted from *Proofs of Christianity* by Donald F. Johns
© 1965 by the Gospel Publishing House. All rights reserved.
Library of Congress Catalog Card Number 77-77215
ISBN 0-88243-911-1
Printed in the United States of America.

A teacher's guide for individual or group study with this book is
available from the Gospel Publishing House. Order Number 32-
0181.

Contents

Contents

1 Faith as a Fact of Life

Romans 1:18-23

Who Believes Anyway?

Two university upperclassmen discussed the question of the existence of God. John, a young Christian studying math, tried hard to convince Bill, a philosophy major, that there is indeed a God. John's reasoning was so forceful that Bill seemed to be losing the argument.

Finally in exasperation Bill protested, "John, the Lord knows I do not believe in God!" Thus he unintentionally demonstrated the difficulty of maintaining the position of a doubter.

Most people would classify Bill as an "unbeliever." However, this means simply he does not believe in God, not that he does not believe in anything at all. All men believe in something, whether they believe in God or not.

Faith is a fact of life. To function sensibly in life a person must trust other people, his automobile, his bank, the pilot of his plane, and countless other things.

Besides the obvious in matters of faith, a person must also place confidence in some overall world-and-life view of things. His philosophy ties the various facets of his personality together and gives him an undergirding foundation on which to build a purposeful life.

Is Faith Folly?

Why, then, do some think a thing like faith is beneath the dignity of informed men? Is faith indeed an illogical quality in life? On the contrary, those who say that belief is unnecessary for men of the world are themselves acting illogically. Their position can be disproved by what is known as the indirect argument in logic:

1. Some people claim that belief in anything is unnecessary.

2. But this is itself a belief.

3. Therefore, on the basis of the claim that belief in anything is unnecessary, belief in the claim itself is self-contradictory.

So everyone believes in something. The question is not: "Shall I believe?" The question is rather: "*What* shall I believe?"

Sources of Truth

Proposed answers come from different directions. Some say men should trust only in truth established by the senses. Such a position is known as empiricism. Others suggest a person is safe to rely on nothing except what reason teaches as truth. They are called rationalists. A third group holds that modern science has all the answers for man in life. In simplicity they see scientists as being authorities on everything just because they have knowledge of some things. This approach to truth is known as scientism.

Can I not know what to believe, then? The fact is, truth exists totally apart from human experience. What is true has that quality whether anyone believes it or not. What is not true is false though all men on earth declare it a fact. That being the case, what path is an individual to follow in his search for truth? Is he to trust his senses, reason, or science to help him discover the facts? Or, are there alternate routes to truth?

Fortunately, there are other sources of truth in the world, and the Bible is the greatest among them. It has the answers to all of the big questions of life, though it may not tell everything one would like to know. For instance, it does not pretend to be a scientific textbook, but it certainly tells man all about himself as a sinner and all he needs to know of God as a holy Being. Then it shows the way to bridge the gap between the two.

Some may say: "But it takes faith to believe what the Bible says is true." No matter, faith is also required to trust the senses, reason, or science to lead to truth. It's what your faith is based on that is important. In time you learn it's unsafe to place your complete trust in anything but the Bible as a source of basic truth.

Seeing and Believing

Acknowledging that God cannot be directly contacted by any of the five senses, is it foolish to believe He exists? The empiricist answers, "Yes." Ultimately, according to the way he views things, all knowledge is reducible to what a person hears, sees, feels, tastes, or smells. An example of this position is the Russian cosmonaut who declared God does not exist because he did not see Him while he was in orbit in outer space.

How safe is it to trust the senses to guide one through life? Certainly, a person can't ignore the testimony of the senses in the knowledge-getting process, because much information comes to him through that medium.

The Bible recognizes the role of the senses in discovering truth. David extends an invitation aimed figuratively at the senses: "O taste and see that the Lord is good" (Psalm 34:8). He also declares that the teachings of the Lord are sweeter than honey (19:10). One of the sayings of Jesus proclaims: "Blessed are the pure in heart: for they shall see God" (Matthew 5:8).

Peter appealed to empirical evidence when testifying about the transfiguration of Jesus. He claimed to be an eyewitness and to have heard the voice of God at that great event (2 Peter 1:16, 18).

John likewise appealed to sensory evidence in referring to his experiences with Jesus. He spoke of that "which we have heard, which we have seen with our eyes, which we have looked upon, and our hands have handled, of the Word of life" (1 John 1:1).

Believing and Not Seeing

Men do learn much through the senses, but the error of empiricism is that it goes too far. It claims *all* knowledge is ultimately derived from the senses. Further, it ignores the fact that the senses are sometimes untrustworthy. The panic-stricken desert traveler whose canteen is empty "sees" an oasis ahead. When he arrives at the spot, though, his eyes reveal nothing but burning sand.

Isaiah's experiences taught him that distorted sensory knowledge can hinder an individual in efforts to arrive at truth. A message from God came to him: "Go, and tell this people, Hear ye indeed, but understand not; and see ye indeed, but perceive not" (Isaiah 6:9).

Empiricism also makes the mistake of not recognizing there are other ways to learn besides through the senses. If I refuse to believe anything except what I experience as truth personally, I am not likely to know much in life. I must generally accept the testimony of past authorities in any field of knowledge about what they have discovered to be true.

Faith as the Sixth Sense

Another means to finding truth is intuition. It is this that gives man a direct knowledge of God's existence. Something within declares that God is.

Paul speaks of this approach to truth in writing to the Romans. He states: "That which may be known of God is manifest in them; for God hath showed it unto them" (Romans 1:19). He elaborates further in declaring that God by nature writes His law on the hearts of men and gives them a conscience as an indestructible witness of His existence (2:14, 15).

Empiricism also overlooks the fact that some things cannot be learned through the senses. John declares: "No man hath seen God at any time" (John 1:18). His point is that it took the coming of Jesus as a man to reveal to men what God is like.

Then, the error of the empiricist is the error of Thomas who said: "Except I shall see . . . , I will not believe" (20:25). Jesus later rebuked his empiricism by saying: "Thomas, because thou hast seen me, thou hast believed: blessed are they that have not seen, and yet have believed" (v. 29).

Scientific Truth

If one concludes that he cannot totally trust his own senses to lead him to truth and therefore must turn to some authority for help, which one is he to lean on?

Many modern people rely on scientists. They have produced so many things to relieve man's misery that it seems safe to follow their leading in all of life's ways. That much of their knowledge is truth and that their facts work well in many areas is undeniable.

However, when we move out of the material realm of life to the area of values and ethics, the scientist is less qualified to speak than other authorities. Many scientists, in fact, have not observed the Almighty in the wonders of His creation as He intends. (Read what Paul writes in Romans 1:20.)

Not only do some scientists fail to see God in nature, but they declare that faith in God is unscientific. They view the method of science as the only way of obtaining knowledge. They are apt to hold to the philosophy of the naturalistic scientist who declares: "Whatever exists, exists in some degree, and can be measured." Since God is not measurable by scientific methodology, they falsely conclude He does not exist.

Professor Cornelius Benjamin of the University of Missouri has defined science as "the method of confirmed hypotheses." A hypothesis is a theory that is advanced to explain certain observed facts.

As a method, science seeks to test its theories. A hypothesis that seems to pass a test of observation is accorded a measure of confirmation. But in science, a hypothesis is never regarded as conclusively proven. A possibility always remains that some other hypothesis will do a better job of explaining the facts.

An example of this is Newton's theory of gravitation. This theory was regarded as the most perfectly established of scientific laws for over two centuries. Yet, it was superseded by Einstein's theory of relativity. More recently a chance theory of atomism has been proposed to replace that.

It is clear, then, that when science claims to present all the truth it is failing to recognize the limitations of its own method of confirmed hypotheses. Science does not present absolute truth, but tentative approximations of the truth which may later have to be revised. It does not present all the truth because it is capable of discovering only that truth that can be measured quantitatively.

When science fails to recognize its own limitations, it is no longer science. It then becomes philosophy. It may even be called a "religion" because the person who falls into the trap of scientism places the same kind of faith in science that others place in God.

The scientific method is suitable for gathering knowledge about God's creation, but not for finding knowledge about God himself. To gather knowledge about God himself, one must have faith.

The knowledge that comes through faith we could call faith-knowledge. It is knowledge that is, in a sense, self-evident. It is knowledge we may have apart from any direct, personal experience. As the writer of Hebrews says: "Through faith we understand that the worlds were framed by the word of God, so that the things which are seen were not made of things which do appear" (11:3).

Trustworthy Reason

If an individual cannot totally trust his senses or the theories of the scientist, to what extent is it safe to place confidence in his own reasoning abilities to distinguish between truth and error? There is ample evidence that the mind of man is a marvelous machine. The life of Helen Keller demonstrates that

one with most of his senses impaired can still become an educated person by diligent application of
the mind.

Man's Maker is the creator of the mind and obviously intended that he use it. Adam made good use
of his mind in the beginning when he gave meaning-
ful names to all the other creatures God had made
(Genesis 2:19).

However, soon after the Fall, man began to misuse
his powers of reason. Recalling the story, Paul says
that men "became vain in their imaginations, and
their foolish heart was darkened. Professing themselves to be wise, they became fools, and changed
the glory of the uncorruptible God . . . to corruptible
man, and to birds, and four-footed beasts, and creep-
ing things" (Romans 1:21-23). Thus they changed
the truth of God into a lie and began to worship the
creature rather than the Creator.

They were not unlike the rationalists of modern
times who claim that belief in God is contrary to
reason. According to them, no "intelligent" person
believes in God.

Foolish Wisdom

To arrive at the belief that there is no God, men
must suppress the truth of which they are intuitively
aware, as well as that to which nature bears witness.
A person taking such a position, as the Psalmist says,
"hath left off to be wise, and to do good" (Psalm
36:3). Or, to put it more plainly: "The fool hath said
in his heart, There is no God" (14:1). The wise man
of old correctly declared: "The fear of the LORD is the
beginning of wisdom" (Proverbs 9:10).

Belief in God is not irrational, but it does at times
go beyond reason and requires faith. One does not

arrive at a belief in the existence of God through reason alone. In fact, since the fall of man, unaided human reason cannot comprehend the truths of God. Paul writes: "But the natural man receiveth not the things of the Spirit of God: for they are foolishness unto him: neither can he know them, because they are spiritually discerned" (1 Corinthians 2:14).

It takes the help of the Spirit for one to know God. Recognizing this, Jesus on one occasion prayed: "I thank thee, O Father, Lord of heaven and earth, because thou hast hid these things from the wise and prudent, and hast revealed them unto babes" (Matthew 11:25). This is humbling to the man who wishes to take undue pride in his intellect, but it is glorifying to God. That, of course, is the very reason God planned it all as He did.

Basic Sin

What shall we say to all of this? We must recognize that the search for truth is not confined to the realm of the intellect. Truth and error stand so opposed to each other that the Bible views them as at war. Consequently, spiritual forces as well as the minds of men are engaged in the struggle.

Efforts to convert men to Christianity involve more than just getting them to change their minds about what they believe. Satan, "the god of this world hath blinded the minds of them which believe not, lest the light of the glorious gospel of Christ, who is the image of God, should shine unto them" (2 Corinthians 4:4). By blinding men's minds, he keeps them from seeing how foolish they are when they reject God's witness in the Bible and in nature. He makes them think they are wise when they hold to the teachings of empiricism, scientism, and rationalism.

All the while, though, they commit the basic sin of unbelief. "He that cometh to God must believe that he is" (Hebrews 11:6). The theologian Henry C. Thiessen views sin as being essentially selfishness. Augustine held that the basic sin is pride. Luther regarded its essence to be unbelief.

Their positions are probably more complementary than contradictory. Unbelief does seem to be at the heart of all sin, yet the disease of doubt may manifest itself in various specific symptoms. In the following chapters you will see how unbelief appears in the form of attacks against the Bible and revelation, attacks against specific Biblical doctrines, and attacks against Christian experience.

2 The Right Religion

Colossians 2:8-23

Alternate Routes to Heaven

Some time ago a young man from a Christian home heard his high school teacher say any religion that causes men to aspire to better things in life is good. No doubt the teacher was repeating what she had been taught at a secular university. The teenager went home and likewise declared what he had heard to his parents and friends without seriously considering the impact of the statement. Not until years later did he come to thoughtfully analyze the proposition that all religions are equally good.

Jesus once discussed the subject of alternate routes to heaven. In the Sermon on the Mount He spoke of two roads (Matthew 7:13, 14). He described a strait gate and a narrow way leading to life. But He also pictured a wide gate and a broad way leading to destruction. Thus, according to Jesus, there is one way to heaven.

Among those who go through the wide gate and along the broad way are the rationalists, the empiricists, and the believers in scientism. Making no pretense about being religious, they boldly proclaim, "There is no God." Their theoretical atheism makes them easy to recognize.

There are other prophets of error on the road to destruction who are not so easily recognized. Their attack on faith is more subtle. Often they profess to believe in God. Sometimes they even claim to be teachers of spiritual truth. Included among them are those who promote syncretism, materialism, and secularism. Of their teachings the wise man of old said: "There is a way which seemeth right unto a man; but the end thereof are the ways of death" (Proverbs 14:12).

Taking the Easy Road

Offering perhaps the easiest road to bliss is the syncretist. What does he teach?

The original meaning of the term *syncretism* is not so bad. It was coined by the Greek Plutarch to speak of the instinct of self-defense that causes people to forget private differences in the face of threats of destruction from without. He applied it to the Cretans who easily quarreled with each other but quickly united when a foreign foe attacked.

However, in time syncretism came to speak of a blending of religious ideas by means of compromise. Either one group adopts the principles and practices of the other or the ways of both are fused into something new.

In former days syncretism was advocated when one nation conquered another. The people of a defeated foe were invited to either recognize their own gods under the names of foreign deities or to welcome the gods of their conquerors as allies. In this manner Zeus of the Greeks was identified with Jupiter of the Romans.

To Agree or Disagree?

These tendencies to inclusivism in matters of religion were prevalent in both Old and New Testament times. How did God view the matter?

From the beginning the Israelites were warned not to assimilate the religion of the Canaanites if they expected the continuing favor of God. Speaking of heathen religious practices Moses warned: "When thou art come into the land which the Lord thy God giveth thee, thou shalt not learn to do after the abominations of those nations" (Deuteronomy 18:9).

Solomon's tendencies to fuse the worship of foreign gods with his own is condemned in Scripture. Noting that his wives turned his head after other gods, the Bible says: "For Solomon went after Ashtoreth the goddess of the Zidonians, and after Milcom the abomination of the Ammonites" (1 Kings 11:5).

The New Testament Church strongly resisted the efforts of early Gnostics to combine Oriental mystery religions, Greek philosophical concepts, and Judaism with Christianity. Paul instructs the Colossians that mystical practices don't belong in the Church: "Let no man beguile you of your reward in a voluntary humility and worshiping of angels" (2:18).

Nor is there a place in the Church for philosophical speculation. Paul continues: "Beware lest any spoil you through philosophy and vain deceit" (v. 8).

The apostle rejects any offer of compromise even with Judaism: "Let no man therefore judge you in meat, or in drink, or in respect of a holy-day, or of the new moon, or of the sabbath days" (v. 16).

In the Church, Christ is all. Of the Christians at Colossae Paul concludes: "And ye are complete in him" (v. 10).

East Meets West

But the syncretist of old still lives. More recent movements to combine religions include the efforts of Theosophy, Bahaism, transcendental meditation, and ecumenism.

Inherent in all except the last of these four movements is a clear attempt to bridge the gap between Eastern and Western philosophies. Theosophy, for example, has served as a pioneer in acquainting the West with the thoughts of the East. Its effectiveness in the 20th-century revival of Buddhism and Hinduism is notable.

Theosophy's one stated purpose is to encourage the study of comparative religions. It claims not to offer a new religion, but a way to understand the universal concepts of God, nature, and man known to wise men of all faiths through the ages.

Likewise, Bahaism says that God has revealed himself through Abraham, Moses, Zoroaster, Jesus, Muhammad, and Baber. All of these are manifestations of His will and teachers of His Word.

Followers of Bahaism proclaim the necessity and inevitability of the unification of all mankind. They see their administrative structure as constituting a blueprint for a future world order. They actively promote the creation or selection of an international language as the beginning step to universal government.

The Bible shows that the promotion of a world religion and a world government is basic to the spirit of the Antichrist. Thus, movements like Bahaism help set the stage for his coming.

TM—Science or Religion?

The most popular of the Eastern religions making inroads in the West is transcendental meditation, or TM, as it is commonly called. A surface definition of TM pictures it as a natural practice of relaxation for two 20-minute periods each day. During the process one repeats a word, known as a *mantra,* in such a way that its rhythmic repetition aids the relaxation effort.

The promoters of TM present it as a "scientific" practice based on biological and psychological laws. They repeatedly declare that it is a nonreligious activity in which men of all faiths may participate with great benefit.

However, an in-depth study of transcendental meditation reveals that it is more than a relaxation tool. It is a religious activity.

Transcendental meditation has its roots in Hinduism. All of its teachings about reality, God, man, and salvation are from the Vedas, the scriptures of the Hindus. The inclusion of the ritualistic initiation ceremony and the use of the secret *mantra* in TM are in keeping with the mystical practices of the cults of the East. Maharishi, world leader of TM, explains the benefits of the technique in religious rather than scientific language.

Meditation as Worship

In Hinduism meditation has enjoyed considerable attention as a means of worship throughout the centuries. In TM it is emphasized as the best means of "transcending" or experiencing unity with God, Being, or Creative Intelligence as the literature of TM refers to Him.

In the view of Maharishi, all creation is one with Being. He illustrates his pantheistic view by declaring that Being permeates all that exists, as butter permeates milk or as sap permeates a tree. Accordingly, this all-pervading, impersonal god-force dwells in the heart of every man.

However, general ignorance of these facts is the

sole source of all man's problems. TM advocates claim one must come to know and experience himself as a part of the whole life of the universe. His relationship to universal life is like that of an individual cell to a whole body.

Maharishi's technique for contacting divine consciousness within, of course, is transcendental meditation.

On Saving Oneself

The theology of TM is called the Science of Creative Intelligence or SCI. The Christian rejects its teachings because SCI denies the Creator-creature distinction fundamental to Biblical revelation.

Contrary to the pantheistic premise of SCI that God is all and all is God, the Bible teaches that God is distinct from His creation. Creation is but the handiwork of God (Psalm 19:1). In confusing God with creation SCI repeats the sin of early man (Romans 1:23, 25).

The doctrine of SCI presents no concept of man's need of a mediator. He becomes his own savior through merely practicing TM.

The Mother Religion

In spite of the fact that its teachings are so different from those of Christianity, Maharishi claims that Christians or followers of any religion may practice TM without conflict. This is because he operates from a Hindu base which has myriads of gods in its theology. To accept one more creates no problem. He says it matters little what name one gives his religion or what ritual he follows in his church, temple, mosque, or pagoda.

It is the Maharishi's view that Hinduism covers

the world's religions by its giant umbrella. Accordingly, the Hindu is the most religiously tolerant of all men on earth. To him the Vedas are the oldest of the scriptures. Whatever truth the sacred books of the world contain appeared first in the Vedas. Thus the basic truth of one religion is the basic truth of all other religions.

Such do-it-yourself religions from the East offer little hope to man. Someone has said they provide at best a set of swimming instructions to a drowning man. Christianity, on the other hand, throws him a life preserver.

Christian Unity

However, not all syncretism is outside the Church. It has appeared recently in Christendom in the form of ecumenism. Presently, ecumenical circles include Protestant, Roman Catholic, and Eastern Orthodox forces. Since 1948 the work of ecumenism has centered in the World Council of Churches.

Ecumenism as a term speaks of a movement toward total-church unity. It seeks to chart a converging course of merging churches and denominations to ultimately achieve its goal. The urge for unity stems from a desire for the Church to exert a greater influence on world affairs, politically, economically, socially, and spiritually. This is seen as the way to establish the kingdom of God on earth and to recapture the heart of unbelieving man.

The eagerness of the movement for unity leads it to minimize the importance of doctrine. It seeks to unite in one fellowship those who believe the Bible is infallible and those who do not believe it; those who believe in miracles and those who do not; and those who believe in the Virgin Birth and the resurrection of Jesus as well as those who do not.

Paul warns the Corinthians against such ecumenical efforts: "Be ye not unequally yoked together with unbelievers: for what fellowship hath righteousness with unrighteousness? and what communion hath light with darkness? and what concord hath Christ with Belial? or what part hath he that believeth with an infidel?" (2 Corinthians 6:14, 15).

Making the Spiritual Material

Joining those of syncretic persuasion as prophets of error in our times are the materialists and the secularists. These terms do not indicate particular religious groups, but rather speak of tendencies found among many.

Currently men are influenced by both philosophical and practical materialists. As a philosophy materialism believes that matter constitutes the only reality there is. It may be reducible to electrons, protons, mesons, or energy or natural laws, but nothing immaterial exists.

Materialists even say man is just a physical being. He has no soul, no spirit, and no "mind." Mental processes are dependent entirely on material actions. The Bible pictures man as having both physical and nonphysical attributes.

Communism is an example of philosophical materialism. Sometimes it is called "dialectical materialism." This term suggests that conflicts of interest over material well-being rightfully force changes in the economic base of society, and therefore in society itself. In other words, social changes are grounded in material values.

Satisfaction Not Guaranteed

Practical materialism is concerned primarily with sensuous pleasure and bodily comforts in this life. It lives with a driving desire to gain more and more material possessions only to find that the more you get the more you want.

Jesus dealt a mighty blow to practical materialism on one occasion. A man asked that the Master command a rich brother to divide his goods with him. Jesus replied: "A man's life consisteth not in the abundance of the things which he possesseth" (Luke 12:15).

The Here and Now

Secularism also has its philosophical and practical elements. In philosophy it is a movement directed away from otherworldliness to this-worldliness.

Philosophical secularism is founded on principles of natural morality independent of revealed religion. Its system of ethics is developed without reference to God or a future life. Man is wholly ruled by natural laws. Therefore his duty is to study them and live by them. Secularism proposes to fulfill the function of religion apart from religion.

Scripture shows that any such self-righteousness is repugnant to God. Isaiah declares: "All our righteousnesses are as filthy rags" (Isaiah 64:6).

Practical secularism may admit the desirability of religion, but sees it as irrelevant to daily living. It divides life into two parts, the sacred and the secular, and believes what happens in one part is unrelated to what happens in the other. What you do in church, that's sacred; what you do outside of church, that's secular. Neither affects the other.

The Bible teaches that *all* of life is sacred, not just a part of it. Paul writes: "Whether therefore ye eat, or drink, or whatsoever ye do, do all to the glory of God" (1 Corinthians 10:31).

Why the Problem?

One sometimes feels it would be wonderful if there was but one religion to which all could subscribe. However, man's dilemma in choosing alternatives in religion has been with him from the beginning.

Eve had to decide whether to believe God or Satan. The Israelites had to choose whether to worship Jehovah or the false gods of the nations around them. Men of the first century were compelled to select the teachings of Christ or those of the Greek philosophers, the Roman gods, the Pharisees, the Sadducees, the Essenes, or the mystery religions of the East.

We do well to note the warning of Jesus in the Sermon on the Mount: "Beware of false prophets, which come to you in sheep's clothing, but inwardly they are ravening wolves" (Matthew 7:15).

3   One of a Kind

2 Timothy 3:14-17

What's in It for You?

A prelaw college student found the campus bookstore out of the required text in one of his courses. The first day in class the professor suggested reading the Bible until the needed books arrived. He meant, of course, that his pupils read the law of Moses. Instead, being ignorant of the contents of the Bible, the young man began reading the Book of Revelation. There he found an emphasis on Christ and was converted. He later became an outstanding minister of the gospel.

This young man was introduced to a study of the Bible in a most unusual way. His teacher directed him to read it because of the information it contains on the subject of law.

The Bible's supreme value, though, lies in its spiritual truths. It is the only Book in the world that tells man how to find peace with God through Jesus Christ. It is one of a kind.

Unlike the prelaw college student, Timothy knew the Bible from childhood. Both his mother and grandmother had taught him (2 Timothy 1:5). Paul reminded him that the Scriptures "are able to make thee wise unto salvation through faith which is in Christ Jesus" (3:15).

A Difference of Opinion

Unfortunately, not all men view the Bible with a respect equal to Paul's. Take the atheists, for example. Whether they are rationalists teaching that belief in God is contrary to reason, believers in scientism teaching that belief in God is unscientific, or empiricists teaching that there is no sensory evidence for the existence of God, they deny that God exists. And since they believe there is no God, they reject the Bible as the Word of God.

However, not all erroneous approaches involve outright rejection of the Bible as the Word of God. Syncretists, emphasizing that all religions have a divine origin and may be reconciled in a universal religion, may view the Bible as one revelation among many. Certainly, they will not admit that it is the unique, distinctive Word of God.

Practical materialism, unlike philosophical materialism which is atheistic, may admit that God exists. However, because it rejects the possibility of prophecy, miracles, and other intrusions of divine power in the world of nature, practical materialism denies that the whole Bible is the Word of God. In theory, practical secularism may admit that the Bible is the Word of God, but in practice it denies it.

Then, there are the humanists who hold that the Bible is a remarkable book, but produced without divine intervention. The modernists, on the other hand, may admit parts of the Scriptures are the Word of God while other segments are uninspired and full of error. Somewhat different from either of these, the neoorthodoxists declare that the Bible becomes the Word of God to the individual only through personal experience.

Man, the Measure of All Things

To look at these last three groups more closely, consider the humanists. Humanism as we know it today came into being during the Renaissance, which ended the Middle or Dark Ages. The Renaissance, meaning "rebirth," was a rebirth of culture and learning. Men began to think for themselves again after having blindly followed the authority of the Roman Catholic Church for about 800 years.

Two movements rejecting the authority of the Roman Catholic Church developed about the same time, Protestantism and humanism. Protestantism accepted the authority of the Bible while rejecting the authority of the Roman Catholic Church. Humanism rejected the authority of both and viewed man as the measure of all things, accepting no authority apart from human reason.

During the Renaissance the humanists rediscovered an emphasis on the nobility of man in his natural state in the classical literature of the Greeks. This led to a rejection of the teachings of the Church on the depravity of man. Humanists declared man is good and capable of solving his own problems in life. Accordingly, his aim in this world should be to develop his potential to the fullest. He should learn to "be himself." His basic aim should be to improve his own lot and that of others on earth. He should do this for the sake of enjoyment in this present world and with no thought of future reward.

Natural Inspiration

In the humanistic view of the origin of the Bible there is an undue emphasis on man's role in the matter. Religious humanists hold that God merely used the natural mental abilities of the writers of Scripture to produce the Bible. Theirs was no more than the inspiration of great authors like Shakespeare. Their insight into spiritual things did not rise above the human level.

This is sometimes referred to as the intuition or genius theory of Biblical inspiration. It is also called natural inspiration, but in a real sense it is not inspiration at all because there is no room in it for the supernatural hand of God in the production of Scripture.

God did use men to write the Bible, but if it is merely a human book, it is subject to error and not trustworthy as an infallible guide for faith and practice. If God exists, then He must be capable of revealing himself to man in such a way that he is certain of receiving the truth.

On Being Sure

God has clearly revealed himself to man. That revelation has come in a general way through nature, history, and conscience. It has appeared in a more special way in miracles, prophecy, and the coming of Christ to earth as a Man.

But none of these things standing alone could accomplish man's salvation. In history God has shown that in the final analysis He rules in the affairs of men. There is sufficient knowledge of God in nature to condemn, but not to save. Conscience is too confusing at times to serve as a dependable guide. Miracles might possibly be faked, and perhaps prophecy can be imitated.

The only way to be sure of God's message to man is through the medium of writing. Without it the world would not even have a dependable record of the birth, death, burial, and resurrection of Jesus as the only means to salvation.

The Bible is more than a human book. Peter declares that no Scripture had its origin in the private will and effort of man: "But holy men of God spake as they were moved by the Holy Ghost" (2 Peter 1:21).

A Modern View

Another low view of the origin of the Bible is that of modernism. It stems from the theories of Charles Darwin in *The Origin of the Species* (Lotowa, NJ: Rowman & Littlefield, Inc., 1972). Upon its publication many concluded that the theory of evolution provided the best explanation of the existence of all material things. They further decided that the theory offered the basis for describing the present advanced stage of things moral, social, cultural, and religious.

The basic assumption modernists drew after Darwin is threefold. The first deduction is that gradual development is the process by which all things came to be. The second is that this development resulted from forces latent in nature without any supernatural assistance. The third is that a comparative method of study alone is sufficient to determine the nature and rate of this development.

Operating on these assumptions, modernists put together what is called the documentary theory of how we got the Bible. According to this evolutionary or developmental theory, the Books of the Bible were compiled from previously existing documents. Take the Pentateuch, for example. It is alleged to have been compiled from four documents: a J document, an E document, a D document, and a P document.

For this reason, the theory is often referred to as "the JEDP theory."

Now it should be emphasized that no one has ever seen the so-called JEDP documents. How did the liberals get the idea that there were documents out of which the Pentateuch was compiled? For one thing, they noticed that two different words were used to name God, Jehovah and Elohim. So they jumped to the conclusion that wherever Jehovah was used to name God, this material came from a document they called the J document (after Jehovah). And wherever God is called Elohim, they concluded this material came from another document they called the E document (after Elohim).

The so-called D document is Deuteronomy, dated by the liberals as being written hundreds of years after Moses. The so-called P document is an alleged priestly code. Anything having to do with priests and priestly works, the liberals arbitrarily assign to it.

Although this evolutionary approach to the Scriptures is most clearly evident with respect to the Pentateuch, it is extended by the liberals to all of the Bible.

The Ancient Record

Obviously, the modernists do not accept the testimony of the Bible at face value. They prefer involved deductions about Biblical authorship instead of the plain statements about authorship from the Bible.

It is true there is no explicit statement in the Pentateuch saying that Moses wrote the entire Pentateuch, but there are many references associating him with large portions of it. He is declared to have recorded the victory over Amalek (Exodus 17:14) and the resting places of Israel during the wilderness journey (Numbers 33:2). He is said to have written the Book of the Covenant (Exodus 20 through 23) and to have composed the hymn and the blessing of Deuteronomy 32 and 33.

Significantly, the materials claimed by the liberals to have come from the so-called P document are said to have been given by the Lord to Moses (Exodus 25:1, 23, 31, for example). Likewise, portions the liberals assign to the so-called D document are said to have been written by Moses (Deuteronomy 31:9, 24-26). The Pentateuch testifies to its having been written by Moses.

Other parts of the Old Testament testify to Mosaic authorship of the Pentateuch (Joshua 1:7; 8:32, 34, 35; 22:5; Judges 3:4; 1 Chronicles 15:15). The New Testament also identifies Moses as the author of the Pentateuch (Mark 12:26; Luke 16:29, 31; John 5:46, 47).

Clearly, the evidence is overwhelming that Moses is the author of the Pentateuch. Once this is admitted, the entire documentary theory of the liberals falls apart, the authorship of the Pentateuch being crucial to it. If the documentary theory is so weak, why do the modernists cling to it so desperately? Obviously, they do not want to admit that the Bible is the inerrant Word of God, and some kind of human authorship is the only alternative left to them.

Getting at the Source

But God, not man, is the source of Scripture. Paul declares this in 2 Timothy 3:16. The implication of his statement is that the very words of the Bible were breathed out by God. Its message is from the mouth of the Lord.

The writers of Scripture themselves do not claim to be the source of their message. In fact, the contrary is true. For example, Paul disclaims originating his message. (Read Galatians 1:11, 12).

Men who did the actual writing of the Bible were but agents of God. The message they wrote was so completely God's that in some instances the writers did not fully understand what they wrote (read 1 Peter 1:10, 11). To write an intelligible message that one does not fully understand certainly requires the miracle of divine inspiration.

The New and the Old

A third erroneous view of the nature of the Bible is that of neoorthodoxy. *Neo* means "new," and *orthodoxy* refers to "right doctrine." The term, then, suggests a school of thought that presents in a new light something that has been around for a long time.

Neoorthodoxy is a new form of liberalism that projects itself as returning to the old paths of Christianity. Originally all liberals held a common optimistic view of life based on a belief in the inherent goodness of man and the ultimate authority of human reason.

However, two world wars in the 20th century jarred the thinking of many liberals about their basic assumptions. How could man be inherently good in the face of devastation at his hands in war? As a result, neoorthodoxy developed in reaction to the evolutionary optimism of the older liberalism.

Its leaders called for a renewed emphasis on the Biblical view of the inherent sinfulness of man. Because of man's sinfulness, it is not safe to trust human reason as the ultimate authority in life. Only divine revelation will do.

Experiencing the Bible

This call for a return to the Bible for divine revelation looks good at first. Regrettably, further study reveals that neoorthodoxy's view of the Bible is not sound. It clings to the documentary theory of other liberals. Furthermore, it holds that Scripture itself is not the Word of God. It *becomes* the word of the Lord only through individual experience.

It is true that the Holy Spirit "makes the Bible real" from time to time as one reads it. However, the mistake of neoorthodoxy is the confusion of "illumination" with "inspiration." The Lord grants illumination of Scripture to all who read it, but the kind of inspiration He gave the writers of the Bible only they will ever know.

If the words of the Bible are not to be considered trustworthy in themselves, how can they be considered trustworthy in conveying the message of God in some crisis experience of an individual? Who determines what part of Scripture is the Word of God? Is each person left alone to be the sole judge? To say the authority of the Bible is dependent on personal experience is to reduce religion totally to subjectivism.

The truth is the Bible is authoritative whether one has a divine encounter with God through it or not. It is authoritative whether one believes it or not. It will rise up on judgment day to condemn man regardless of his opinion of it. Wholly apart from any particular individual's reaction to the Bible, it is the Word of God.

4   It Is Enough

2 Peter 1:12-21

Lost-and-found Department

The curiosity of a young convert was greatly aroused when a neighbor gave him a "lost book of the Bible." The book pictured Jesus as a lad bringing real life to a pigeon He had formed out of clay. It showed Him being worshiped by the animals of the woods. When one cut a board too short in Joseph's carpenter shop, Jesus lengthened it with a word.

But curiosity turned to serious question when the new Christian found a story of Jesus turning a donkey into a man in the book. Real doubt as to the authenticity of the "lost gospel" arose when he read of the boy Jesus killing a playmate for mutilating some items He had carved out of mud. It helped little that the story ended with the resurrection of the lad.

Study with the passing of the years led the young Christian to discard such books and to conclude that the Bible is complete as is. Nothing more needs to be added. It is enough.

No More and No Less

Men commit two errors in their approach to Scripture. Some want to take away from it. Those who deny that the Bible in total is God's Word in effect do this. The humanists, modernists, and neoorthodoxists seek to subtract from Scripture in this way.

Others admit that the Bible is the Word of God in some sense, but refuse to admit it is unique and complete. They commit the sin of wanting to add to Scripture. Among them are the Mormons, Jehovah's Witnesses, Christian Scientists, and even Roman Catholics.

The Christian must avoid both errors. He needs only the completed canon of Scripture to show him the path to God. The 66 Books of the Bible, no more and no less, constitute God's Word.

Gold-plated Revelation

However, Mormons are not of this opinion. They believe the Bible is not enough. Something more is needed. Thus they have supplied additional books. The Book of Mormon is among them. Its author is Joseph Smith, founder of Mormonism.

The background of Mr. Smith is that of a treasure hunter. His skills as a youth included those of locating lost objects by means of a "Peek Stone." He claimed supernatural powers resided in the "Stone."

Mr. Smith's greatest "find" turned out to be that of the golden plates on which the Book of Mormon was allegedly written. Reportedly, he unearthed the plates in 1827 near Palmyra, New York.

The translation of the plates from "reformed Egyptian hieroglyphics" took place behind a curtain where Mr. Smith and the mysterious documents were screened off from the view of others. Supposedly, he was the only human being to ever see the plates. Once the translation was complete, an angel took the plates back to heaven.

Contradictory Testimony

It seems unlikely that a book of such origin was meant to supplement the Bible. Its story of the two groups who came to people the American continent appears dubious. There is neither anthropological nor archaeological evidence that any such civilizations as they reportedly established ever existed.

Even the story of their coming to America is a strange one. Allegedly, the Jaredites left the Tower of Babel about 2250 B.C. Their means of transportation were "air tight" barges designed by the Lord. When the builders protested that the people would smother in them, the Lord supposedly instructed that a hole be made "in the top *and also in the bottom*" of each barge to unstop periodically that there might be adequate air to breathe!

Mormon theology contradicts what is found in the Bible. Joseph Smith taught that God was once a man, that He has a tangible body of flesh and bones, and that consequently all men may become like God is now. He viewed the Holy Spirit as being a nonperson. Accordingly, Jesus was not begotten by the Spirit, but by the resurrected, glorified Adam-god.

In view of these things, the Christian rejects the Book of Mormon as a supplement to the Bible.

A Key to Scripture

Christian Scientists likewise claim that the message of salvation in the Bible is not sufficient as is. It cannot be read and interpreted literally. According to Mary Baker Eddy, founder of the movement, the material record of Scripture is of no more value to personal well-being than what one finds in a history book. What is important is *Science and Health With*

Key to the Scriptures, published by Mrs. Eddy in 1875.

Mrs. Eddy claims divine inspiration of her book, stating she merely wrote down what God said. Further, she declares that the revelations of her work are higher, clearer, and more permanent than any given before.

Another Gospel

An examination of Mrs. Eddy's teachings shows hers is not a supplement to Scripture, but it is actually another gospel. She rejects such basic Biblical teachings as the Trinity and the deity of Christ.

Following the teachings of Hegel, Mrs. Eddy was an idealist who denied the reality of all things material. Reasoning syllogistically she concluded: God is all. God is mind. Therefore, mind is all.

And further: Mind is all. Matter is not mind. Therefore, matter does not exist.

Thus, she could not accept the teaching of Scripture that God became man in Jesus. God himself is but an impersonal force. Pure Spirit could not join itself to nonexistent matter.

On the same philosophical base, Mrs. Eddy declared that evil and sickness are not real. Since God is good and He is all, there is no room for His opposite in the universe. So men are healed not by merely claiming there is no sickness, but by knowing there is none.

Following this logic to its natural conclusion, death is not real. Thus, according to Mrs. Eddy, Jesus did not actually die on the cross and the Resurrection never occurred. What Jesus did through it all was to demonstrate the power of Spirit to destroy material illusions.

Further, in the view of Mrs. Eddy, since evil does not exist except in the minds of the uninformed, man is not a sinner. He needs no savior. In the mind of God man has always been saved. Obviously, such teachings strike a blow at the very heart of the gospel of Jesus Christ.

Better Than the Bible?

Charles T. Russell, founder of Jehovah's Witnesses, is another who offers a book to add to the Bible. Actually, he presents his *Studies in the Scriptures* (Brooklyn: Watchtower Bible & Tract Soc., 1886-1917) as being better than the Bible. In his view it is safer to leave the Scriptures unread and ponder his book than to study the Bible and ignore what he has written. He warns that to read the Bible alone without his book leads to darkness.

Russell's successor, Judge J. F. Rutherford, was a more prolific writer than the founder of Jehovah's Witnesses. From his pen flowed over 100 books and pamphlets.

Followers of these two men view their writings as more than just commentaries on the Scriptures. To them they are the Bible in an "arranged form," making Scripture plainer than it is in its original context.

Among more recent books Jehovah's Witnesses wish to add to the Bible is *The New World Translation of the Christian Greek Scriptures*. The work's main accomplishment is the alteration of the literal meaning of some Greek words so as to support the movement's denial of the deity of Christ.

Thus the book continues in the tradition of Mr. Russell in his mishandling of the Greek text. Pastor Russell presented himself as an authority on the original languages of Scripture until forced to declare under oath in court that he was totally ignorant of Greek and Hebrew. Individual Jehovah's Witnesses tend yet to leave the false impression that they are students of the original languages of the Bible.

Lacking in Orthodoxy

The literature of Jehovah's Witnesses is totally lacking in orthodoxy. Much of the false teaching centers on Christ.

To the Witnesses Jesus is not God. He is a created being. Nor is the Holy Spirit God. Rather, He is merely God's active force in the universe. Thus there is no Trinity. Jehovah alone is supreme.

Since they deny the deity of Christ, His death has a different meaning from that of orthodox Christianity. So does His resurrection. Witnesses reject the idea of the bodily resurrection of Jesus. He was raised merely as a "spiritual creature." But after His resurrection Jesus said: "Behold my hands and my feet, that it is I myself: handle me, and see; for a spirit hath not flesh and bones, as ye see me have" (Luke 24:39).

Denial of the physical resurrection of Jesus leads Jehovah's Witnesses to refuse the teaching of His bodily return to earth. According to them He actually returned as an invisible, "spiritual creature" in 1914, expelled Satan from heaven, and is now establishing the Theocratic Millennial Kingdom. For this reason Witnesses refuse allegiance to any government.

However, these views do not correspond to the plain teachings of Scripture on Christ's return. (Read Acts 1:11.)

Further, false concepts of the death and resurrection of Jesus result in erroneous teachings among Witnesses on these events for all men. For them the

39

soul of man is not eternal but mortal. It can die. In death, the soul sleeps. In the resurrection the souls of all who have rejected Jehovah will be annihilated. Therefore, there is no hell.

Jesus viewed things differently. To His followers He said: "Fear not them which kill the body, but are not able to kill the soul: but rather fear him which is able to destroy both soul and body in hell" (Matthew 10:28).

Roman Scriptures

Even Roman Catholics add to Scripture. True, they accept the Bible as the Word of God as do Protestants. But whereas Protestants rely solely on the Word of God as their authority in spiritual things, Roman Catholics believe that the decisions of church councils, decisions of the pope in matters of faith and morals, and tradition supplement the Bible.

Take the doctrine of the veneration of Mary, for example. The Bible simply speaks of Mary as blessed (literally, well spoken of) among women (Luke 1:28). In 431 A. D., however, the Council of Ephesus applied the title "Mother of God" to her. Soon the devotion accorded to her was but little short of that given to God. Prayers were offered to her, asking her to intercede with her Son on man's behalf.

Writers began saying she had never committed an act of sin and that she remained a virgin perpetually. In 1854, Pius IX declared her to have been immaculately conceived in such a way as to have been preserved from any taint of original sin. In 1950, Pius XII proclaimed the assumption of Mary, meaning she was taken bodily into heaven. Roman Catholics believe she is now in heaven using her influence with Jesus on behalf of those who pray to her.

Should a Roman Catholic be pressed as to the truthfulness of these doctrines which are not contained in the Bible, he would probably claim that although the doctrines themselves are not in Scripture, their seeds are. He might go on to say the world has the Bible only because the Roman Catholic Church gave it to men. The implication of this claim is obvious: the authority of the Roman Catholic Church is greater than the authority of the Bible.

What of the claim that the Roman Catholic Church gave the world the Bible? The Books of the Bible existed and were used by Christians long before Rome gained any authority over churches established elsewhere. In fact, by the last half of the second century there was a fair degree of agreement among Christians as to what books were spiritually useful. They recognized that there was something about those particular books that enabled the Holy Spirit to speak to their hearts in a special way.

Athanasius, bishop of Alexandria, in an Easter letter written in 367, mentioned the 27 Books now included in the New Testament. (At this time, the church at Alexandria had a degree of authority equal to that of the church at Rome.) The Council of Hippo in 393, and the Council of Carthage in 397, recognized the same 27 Books already in use as Holy Scripture.

These councils did not enact legislation declaring these to be Scripture, but acknowledged them to already be in use as Scripture by Christians everywhere. All of this happened before 451, the year Leo the bishop of Rome made his power grab which resulted in the bishops of Rome being recognized as successors of Peter and as ranking above all the other bishops of the Church. It was not until 1546 at the Council of Trent, after the beginnings of the Protestant Reformation, that the Roman Catholic Church designated its canon—and at the same time formally gave tradition equal weight.

Peter indicates that the Books of the Old and New Testaments constitute the Word of God (2 Peter 1:12-21). He speaks of the first 39 Books of the Bible as a "sure word of prophecy" which men do well to heed. At the same time Peter shows that God meant his writings, with those of other apostles, to be preserved after their deaths as additional Scripture. Peter declares they contain no "cunningly devised fables," but the truth of God. These writings men now have in the last 27 Books of the Bible.

No More to Tell

The 66 Books of Scripture contain a revelation of all that is necessary for man's salvation. The Old Testament shows man as a sinner in need of a Saviour. Then it points to the coming of Jesus as man's Redeemer. The four Gospels tell of Christ's coming as the greatest possible revelation of God to man. The Epistles explain the significance of Jesus' visit to earth. Finally, the Book of Revelation centers on the promise of His return to the world. What more can God say to man? What else is there to tell?

God's Word is a closed Book. It is a completed volume, not a loose-leaf notebook. The Bible contains warnings against adding to or subtracting from its contents. These appear in the beginning (Deuteronomy 4:2), middle (Proverbs 30:6), and end (Revelation 22:18, 19) of the Book.

5 Looking Ahead

Isaiah 41:21-29

Getting Out on a Limb

Without divine guidance, predicting the future is risky business!

A self-styled prophet stood in a religious meeting with a forecast of the future in his area. He declared that tragedy would soon come to the city of 100,000 in the Midwest where he lived. Its destruction would be by tornado. The awful event would occur on Friday, October 15, of that year.

The prophet reported a vision as the source of his prediction. In it he saw the fall of specific churches in the town. A Baptist church on the north side of town was among them. A large evangelical church in the center of the city fell too. Bethel Temple on the south side likewise crumbled, with the sole exception of its east wall which was left standing.

The congregation receiving the prophet's message was sobered by what he said. Months passed. Finally, the fateful day arrived. To the relief of all who knew of the predicted destruction, it went by without a cloud in the sky.

The town still stands after years have passed. The churches the prophet said he saw fall continue to grow. Obviously man, not God, was the source of that prophecy.

Predictions in the Bible are quite different from the above. Biblical prophecy contains information beyond the power of human insight. It has sufficient details to preclude mere guesswork. It extends beyond the reach of self-fulfillment. Because their source is the mind of an all-knowing God, many prophecies have already been fulfilled to the smallest detail. Others are now being fulfilled. And you can rest assured those concerning what is yet future will likewise come to pass.

A basic difference between the Bible and other sacred books of the world, such as the Koran and the Vedas, is in the area of prophecy. They have virtually no predictions of the future, while the Bible is full of prophecy. Seventeen of the 39 Books of the Old Testament are prophetic in nature. In the New Testament, whole chapters of the Gospels, extended passages in the Epistles, and the entire Book of Revelation are devoted to prophecy.

Ability to successfully predict future events also distinguished the true God Jehovah from the false gods of Old Testament days. Isaiah challenged them to "show us what will happen," and to "declare us things for to come" (Isaiah 41:22). By this they would prove their existence as genuine gods. Only silence followed his challenge.

In contrast, Isaiah showed Jehovah as one who declares the end from the beginning. Then he boldly predicted the coming of Cyrus to intervene in the affairs of Israel 150 years before the great Persian ruler was born (v. 25).

Later Isaiah called Cyrus by name and gave details concerning his political activities. But this is only one of several examples showing God knows where

He stands when He speaks of future events. Others include Daniel's advance outline of world history, Ezekiel's predictions of the destruction of Tyre, prophecies about the nation of Israel, what the Old Testament says of the coming of Jesus to earth, and details foretold in the Gospels of the fall of Jerusalem in 70 A. D. These fulfilled prophecies serve as evidence that the Bible is the inerrant Word of God.

The Proof Is in the Reading

What Isaiah said about Cyrus long before his birth causes the modernists to question the authenticity of the prophet's Book. In the eighth century B. C. he wrote that Cyrus would give the order to rebuild Jerusalem and the temple (Isaiah 44:28; 45:1). In the sixth century B. C., some 200 years later, the order was actually given by Cyrus (2 Chronicles 36:22, 23; Ezra 1:1-4). Modernists reason that Isaiah could not possibly have had exact knowledge concerning Cyrus in advance, and so conclude that Isaiah did not write that passage of Scripture.

Other predictions of Isaiah also contribute to the debate on the genuineness of his Book. Modernists tend to believe he wrote the first 39 chapters, but an unknown person authored the rest.

In part, it is the modernists' reluctance to admit the possibility of miracles that forces them to take this position. Since the last 27 chapters of Isaiah contain forecasts of events in the distant future, and since such predictions require the miraculous in prophecy, they call the last part of the Book history, written by someone after the events had actually occurred.

However, New Testament writers quote from the last part of the Book of Isaiah and attribute it to

Isaiah (Matthew 3:3; Isaiah 40:3). Jesus does the same (John 12:38; Isaiah 53:1). Either Jesus and the New Testament writers are wrong, or the modernists are wrong. The correct choice is clear.

The Doom of a City

Arguments of liberals that Biblical prophecies are really historical records come to an abrupt halt when viewing Ezekiel's prophecy about the city of Tyre. He prophesied in the sixth century B. C. One thing he predicted was an assault on Tyre (Ezekiel 26:7-11). Part of his prophecy was soon fulfilled when Nebuchadnezzar attacked the city. After a 13-year siege, Tyre fell. Before the fall of the city, the people removed their possessions to an island about ½ mile from the mainland and built a new Tyre there. After Nebuchadnezzar took the old city, desolated it, and departed, the people of Tyre made no effort to re-build it.

So far, it might be possible to claim that Ezekiel, living in the time of Nebuchadnezzar, was writing history. But all of Ezekiel's prophecy was not yet fulfilled. He had predicted specifically: "They shall lay thy stones and thy timber and thy dust in the midst of the water" (v. 12). Speaking for the Lord he said further: "And I will make thee like the top of a rock: thou shalt be a place to spread nets upon" (v. 14). Yet, the desolate ruins of the city were still standing. The site of old Tyre was not yet swept clean.

About 2½ centuries passed, and Alexander the Great was conquering the Mediterranean world. When Tyre refused to submit, Alexander took the ruins of the old city of Tyre, put them in the sea, and built a causeway to the new island-city to bring it to its knees. It was then that Ezekiel's prophecy was totally fulfilled. True to the last part of the prophet's message, mainland Tyre has never been rebuilt (v. 14).

Reviving a Nation

More positive proof that Biblical prophecy is a miracle of heaven is the nation of Israel. The Old Testament contains numerous predictions of the fall of Israel for sins against Jehovah. Moses was the first to speak of it. He warned: "The Lord shall scatter thee among all people, from the one end of the earth even unto the other. . . . And thy life shall hang in doubt before thee; and thou shalt fear day and night, and shalt have none assurance of thy life" (Deuteronomy 28:64, 66).

Later, Jeremiah gave a similar prediction. (Read Jeremiah 24:9.)

True to the words of these prophets, the people of Israel were driven from the Promised Land and scattered to the four winds. This happened at the Babylonian captivity in the Old Testament and again at the destruction of Jerusalem in 70 A. D.

Yet, the Lord promised a restoration of Israel. Jeremiah said: "Though I make a full end of all nations whither I have scattered thee, yet will I not make a full end of thee" (Jeremiah 30:11). Ezekiel declared: "Behold, I will take the children of Israel from among the heathen, whither they be gone, and will gather them on every side, and bring them into their own land" (Ezekiel 37:21).

Indeed, the nation of Israel was restored after 70 years in Babylonian exile, but only in part. Total national sovereignty did not again belong to the Jews until the miraculous rebirth of the country on May

14, 1948. This second, full restoration of Israel was predicted by Isaiah: "And it shall come to pass in that day, that the Lord shall set his hand again *the second time* to recover the remnant of his people, which shall be left. . . . And [he] shall assemble the outcasts of Israel, and gather together the dispersed of Judah from the four corners of the earth" (Isaiah 11:11, 12).

Too Much to Tell

The greatest indication of the miracle of prophecy concerns the coming of Jesus to earth. The Old Testament contains over 300 predicted details of that event. Nearly 100 of these prophecies are specifically quoted by New Testament writers as proof that Jesus was the Messiah promised to Israel. To refer to all of them would be too much to tell, but the following list presents amazing evidence of the trustworthiness of Biblical prophecy:

1. The Son of God was to be born of the seed of woman (Genesis 3:15). Jesus' birth fulfilled that prophecy (Galatians 4:4).

2. The Messiah was to be born of a virgin (Isaiah 7:14). Jesus was born of the virgin Mary (Matthew 1:22, 23).

3. The Christ was to be a King of the line of David (Jeremiah 23:5). Jesus was King of the Jews and of the house of David (Matthew 2:2; Luke 1:31-33).

4. The Promised One was to be born in Bethlehem (Micah 5:2). Christ was born there (Matthew 2:1-6).

5. God's Son was to receive homage from Gentiles (Isaiah 60:3). Our Lord was worshiped early by the Gentile Wise Men (Matthew 2:1-11).

6. The Messiah was to have a forerunner (Malachi

3:1; 4:5, 6). John the Baptist served as a forerunner for Christ (Mark 1:2-4).

7. The Holy Spirit was to rest in a special way on the Holy One (Isaiah 11:2; 61:1). John the Baptist saw the Spirit descend and remain on Jesus (Luke 3:21, 22; 4:16-19).

8. The Christ was to be a worker of miracles (Isaiah 35:5, 6; 53:4). Matthew 8:16, 17 refers to Jesus in fulfilling this prophecy.

9. The Son of God was not to seek fame (Isaiah 42:1-4). The New Testament notes this modesty of Jesus (Matthew 12:15-21).

10. The Promised One was to have great zeal for the purity of the temple (Psalm 69:9). Twice in His ministry Jesus showed that zeal (John 2:17; Matthew 21:12).

11. The Messiah was to enter Jerusalem as a King riding on a donkey (Zechariah 9:9). Jesus fulfilled this prophecy at the Triumphal Entry (Matthew 21:4, 5).

12. God's Son was to be betrayed by a friend (Psalm 41:9). Judas fulfilled this prophecy (John 13:18). The price of betrayal was to be 30 pieces of silver (Zechariah 11:12), and so it was (Matthew 26:15).

13. The Christ was to be deserted by His companions (Zechariah 13:7). After Jesus was taken prisoner, even the apostles left Him (Matthew 26:56).

14. The Promised One was to be beaten and spat upon (Isaiah 50:6). Jesus was shamefully treated just as predicted (Matthew 26:67; 27:26, 30).

15. The Messiah's garments were to be divided by lot (Psalm 22:18). Soldiers cast lots for the clothing of Jesus (John 19:23, 24).

16. The Son of God was to feel forsaken (Psalm

22:1). Jesus felt that even God had forsaken Him on the cross (Matthew 27:46).

17. The Christ was to experience thirst and be offered vinegar to drink (Psalm 22:15; 69:21). That happened to Jesus (John 19:28; Matthew 27:48).

18. The bones of the Son of God were not to be broken in crucifixion (Psalm 34:20). The bones of Jesus were not broken (John 19:32-36).

19. The Messiah was to be buried in the grave of a rich man (Isaiah 53:9). Jesus was buried in the tomb of the rich Joseph of Arimathea (Matthew 27:57-60).

20. The Promised One was to be raised from the dead (Psalm 16:10). Peter declared that Jesus was that One (Acts 2:31).

The Fall of Jerusalem

The genuineness of Biblical prophecy also appears in its predictions of the fall of Jerusalem in the first century. Matthew, Mark, and Luke contain forecasts of the destruction of Jerusalem (Matthew 24:1-28; Mark 13:1-23; Luke 21:5-24). Modernists' reluctance to admit the possibility of prophecy leads them to view these accounts as historical facts rather than prophetic, so they date these three Gospels after the fall of the city in 70 A. D.

However, traditional views concerning Matthew, Mark, and Luke being the authors of the Gospels bearing their names support dates of authorship before 70 A. D. The reliability of such views is evidenced by the Gospel of Luke.

Luke and Acts were written by the same person (Luke 1:1-4; Acts 1:1). A study of the "we" passages in Acts where the author indicates his presence at events described reveals Luke as that author.

As far as dates are concerned, Acts ends with Paul

still in prison at Rome, probably in 62 or 63 A. D. Since the Gospel of Luke was written prior to Acts, it must have been written about 60 A. D. If Luke's Gospel prophetically foresaw the destruction of Jerusalem 10 years before it happened, there is no reason to believe that Matthew's and Mark's Gospels could not do likewise.

One in a Million

Chances of one in a million don't even begin to allow for Biblical prophecies to be human or accidental predictions. Forecasting a single event of only one detail by the laws of chance affords a 50 percent probability of fulfillment. The event either will or will not happen. Adding one detail reduces the chances of successful prediction to 25 percent. A third detail leaves only one chance in eight of a fulfilled prophecy. With over 300 predicted details of Christ's first coming, there is virtually no chance of any one man at a given point in time being exactly what was foretold.

The Bible is the Word of God and not of man. The miracle of prophecy helps establish that fact. Those who reject prophecy do so mainly because their philosophy of life does not allow for the possibility of miracles.

6 On Seeking Signs

Mark 16:14-20

A Blind Man's Game

It is said that a man convinced against his will is of the same opinion still.

Two neighboring farmers, Mr. Sorenson and Mr. Crabtree, discussed a mutual rodent problem. Mr. Sorenson declared he had more rats under his barn than anyone in the world. Mr. Crabtree expressed doubt. "Come over to my place and I'll show you," was the reply.

Upon arrival at the farm, Mr. Sorenson asked Mr. Crabtree to stand on the opposite side of the barn from him. With a bit of noise the rats would scrabble out the other side, and the dubious farmer would be convinced.

When the experiment was completed, Mr. Sorenson came around the barn and said, "Well, what did I tell you?" Mr. Crabtree simply responded, "I didn't see a thing."

The men took positions on the other two sides of the barn. Mr. Sorenson repeated his efforts to scare the rats out for Mr. Crabtree to see. He vigorously made noises and then dashed around the building to catch a glimpse of the rodents for himself. Suddenly, he discovered why Mr. Crabtree had seen nothing on either try. His neighbor stood silently with both eyes closed!

Insufficient Evidence

People who reject the idea of miracles often ask for evidence. Yet so negative is their attitude that they would reject the evidence even if it were presented. It was the day after the feeding of the 5,000 when the people who had observed the miracle asked: "What sign showest thou then, that we may see, and believe thee?" (John 6:30). And not long after the feeding of the 4,000, the Pharisees and Sadducees asked Jesus for a sign from heaven (Matthew 16:1). No amount of evidence is sufficient to convince the person who does not want to believe.

Belief in the possibility of miracles is related to belief in the existence of God and in the Bible as the Word of God. Those who do not believe in God have no basis for believing in miracles. Those who reject the Bible as God's Word naturally refuse to believe the accounts of miracles contained therein. None of this is surprising, since belief in miracles points to the existence of God and to Jesus as His Son, neither of which the doubter wishes to accept.

Such a position leads skeptics in efforts to explain away the miracles of the Bible. Of all the miracles performed by Jesus, the Gospels list only about 35. People who object to the possibility of miracles have directed their attacks mainly against these. Their explanations center on the supposed simplicity of the spectators, alleged false conclusions based on mere coincidence, a diagnostic insight of Jesus regarding physical illness, an assumption that all Biblical healings were of psychosomatic diseases, or the claim that certain miracles are dramatic allegories rather than true stories.

Offending Mother Nature

Behind all the efforts to explain away the miracles of the Bible is a naturalistic philosophy of life. According to this view, nature constitutes all the reality there is in the universe. Since a miracle may be considered as an event apparently transcending known natural laws, resulting from the intrusion of the supernatural into the world of the natural, it is considered impossible.

The philosopher Hume reasoned from the premise that everything that happens is the result of natural law. Then, since miracles are contrary to natural law, they are impossible. However, his logic is fallacious on several counts.

Natural laws are not iron-clad decrees that determine all universal phenomena. They are rather the creation of men chosen to explain what are considered to be the orderly events of nature. Since they are explanations rather than causes, they serve best by telling us what has happened with reasonable regularity, rather than by setting limits on the possibility of what can happen.

Further, Hume was wrong in picturing the universe as a mere mechanical apparatus operating by innate, impersonal power. God is the author of nature. He also upholds "all things by the word of his power" (Hebrews 1:3). Since He created all and sustains all, any unusual present act of His is not an interruption of natural law, but actually a part of that law. Miracles are but a part of His ongoing activity in the universe. They no more break the laws of nature than the artist "violates" the rules of painting by departing from generally accepted procedures to achieve a special effect.

Simple Spectators

People seek to explain away some miracles by attributing them to the world-view of the spectators. They argue that people of the first century viewed things differently than we do today in the modern scientific age. They were simple, superstitious folk without an understanding of the laws of nature.

For example, what we now view as mental disorder, they then viewed as demon possession. According to this objection, Jesus either was a product of His time with the same erroneous world-view as others, or else He accommodated himself to their erroneous views to meet them on their own level.

More correctly, though, it is the antisupernaturalists who have the wrong conception of the world. There is a God, and there is a world of the unseen behind this physical world. There is such a thing as mental illness, but there is also demon possession. Jesus neither was in error nor did He accommodate himself to error. Besides, to explain the casting out of demons as instantaneous cures of severe mental illness would make the incidents none the less miraculous.

Furthermore, those of the first century who marveled at Jesus' miracles knew them to be beyond the power of anything natural. When He healed the blind man they remarked that this had never happened since the beginning of time (John 9:32). Joseph may not have known as much about genetics as modern man, but he certainly understood that an act of God was necessary for Mary to be pregnant apart from sexual intercourse with a man.

People of the first century were not unlearned, simple, gullible folk. There were sophisticated skeptics then as now. However, one difference is that some of these early opponents were forced to admit the reality of His miracles (Acts 4:16), while many now continue in their efforts to explain them away.

A Mere Coincidence

Another way people try to cast doubt on the genuineness of Jesus' miracles is by attributing them to coincidence. They argue that the mere fact that two things happen at about the same time does not mean one is the cause of the other.

For example, after Jesus spoke to the demon-possessed man, calming him, a herd of swine rushed down into the sea and drowned (Mark 5:1-20). Since no one saw the demons pass into the swine from the demoniac, the idea of transference was a mistaken inference of cause and effect.

It is concluded that either the behavior of the demoniac or the excited behavior of the crowd caused the swine to stampede. However, to explain the miracle by coincidence, one must ignore the sequence of events in the Biblical record. The herd stampeded after the demoniac was calmed, not while he was excited. The crowd became excited after the stampede, not before.

The inadequacy of coincidence as an explanation of miracles may be illustrated by its application to the stilling of the storm. The coincidence theory assumes the wind just happened to cease as Jesus rebuked the disciples (Matthew 8:26), and the disciples mistakenly assumed Jesus had rebuked the wind. While it may be granted that storms come and go with suddenness on the Sea of Galilee, the suddenness here was exceptional. The disciples were more frightened by the stilling of the storm than by the storm itself (Mark 4:40, 41).

Psychological Disorders

Still others try to explain away the miracles of Jesus by focusing on psychological disorders. Their theory stresses that 50 or more percent of those under doctors' care today have symptoms with psychological rather than organic causes. Similar conditions may have existed in the time of Jesus. Thus, many who came to Him for healing may have had psychological problems readily helped by faith rather than physiological problems cured.

Certainly faith in Christ will benefit those who have psychological problems, but many healings performed by Jesus cannot be explained on this basis. He healed a man with a withered hand (Mark 3:5) and a man born blind (John 9:7). Their problems were obviously physiological and not psychological.

C. S. Lewis notes some of the Master's miracles speeded up nature's ordinary processes. Others, however, either resulted in the actual reversal of the laws of nature or were totally contrary to anything "natural." Peter's walk on the water was completely above anything nature has provided for (Matthew 14:28-32). Lazarus' resurrection after being dead 4 days reversed the process of nature (John 11:1-46).

Dramatic Allegory

The raising of Lazarus from the dead presents a real problem to those who do not believe in miracles. Since he was 4 days in the tomb, it cannot be claimed he was in a coma. Yet to admit Lazarus was actually raised would be to admit the possibility of miracles. Here antisupernaturalists develop another theory to dispense with the miraculous in Jesus' ministry.

Skeptics treat the story of Lazarus as if it were not actually historically true. They call it a dramatic allegory, an acted-out parable created by the author of the Gospel of John. Its purpose is to symbolize the truth that Jesus is the resurrection and the life. However, there is not a shred of evidence that can be presented to indicate the story is a dramatic allegory. To call it an allegory does not make it one.

Miraculous Purposes

Sincere seekers soon see the fallacy of theories that seek to explain away the miracles of the Bible. They see the miraculous of both past and present as fitting into God's plan for the ages in relating to man.

The honest inquirer knows that miracles do not exist for their own sake. Rather, they point to the fact that God is at work in a remarkable way in the universe.

Unless a miracle brings one to see Jesus as Saviour, it has failed to achieve its highest purpose.

Neither do miracles occur as magical tricks to entertain the curious. When the scribes and Pharisees said, "Master, we would see a sign from thee" (Matthew 12:38), Jesus refused, rebuking them as part of an evil and adulterous generation.

Nor are miracles given in efforts to convince dedicated unbelievers. Jesus knew such was impossible. He told about a wicked rich man who died and was in torment. The rich man asked Abraham to send the beggar Lazarus to warn his five unbelieving brothers, indicating they would repent if someone miraculously returned from the dead to warn them.

Abraham replied: "If they hear not Moses and the prophets, neither will they be persuaded, though one rose from the dead" (Luke 16:31). In rejecting the writings of the Old Testament, they would refuse the most miraculous of testimony.

Confirming the Word

Miracles serve to confirm the Word of God. The marvelous healing of a paralytic demonstrated the authority of a word from Jesus in forgiving the man his sins (Mark 2:1-12).

In the Great Commission, Jesus said: "These signs shall follow them that believe; In my name shall they cast out devils; they shall speak with new tongues; they shall take up serpents; and if they drink any deadly thing, it shall not hurt them; they shall lay hands on the sick, and they shall recover" (16:17, 18). This is exactly what happened: "They went forth, and preached every where, the Lord working with them, and confirming the word with signs following" (v. 20).

In other words, signs have the same function in the ministry of believers as they had in the ministry of Christ. Miraculous signs confirm the truth of the Word which is preached about Christ, pointing men to Him as the Son of God and the Saviour of their souls.

This is illustrated further in the healing of the man born blind (John 9). Several purposes were accomplished through this miracle. The man received his sight after a life of blindness. The healing also did something for the man's soul. He first concluded that Jesus was a prophet, then he saw Him as Saviour and received Him as such and worshiped Him. There was also a great witness for Christ in the community because of the miracle. People were convinced that Jesus had a special relationship with God and was not the imposter His critics claimed Him to be. Finally, Jesus used the occasion to teach a lesson on spiritual blindness.

Let's Have It Live

Those who reject the miracles of the Bible often present explanations that are harder to believe than the simple record of Scripture. For example, some try to explain the Bible's account of the Flood by saying a meteorite fell into the Mediterranean Sea with a splash sufficient to push Noah's ark atop Mt. Ararat. But what size stone would it take to accomplish that?

Or, others describe the miraculous fire by night and cloud by day that guided the Children of Israel in their journey to the Promised Land in equally strange ways. According to them, the fire was the light of torches carried on high poles by those who led the march. The cloud was the smoke arising from the extinguished torches with the rising of the sun each day.

Why are men so bent on offering a naturalistic interpretation of the miracles of Scripture? A religion without a live, acting God is not worthy to claim its roots in the Bible. In the words of Paul, it has a "form of godliness, but [denies] the power thereof" (2 Timothy 3:5). Its God is dead!

7 Let the Story Stand

Luke 1:26-38

Can It Be True?

All beds in the ward of the mental hospital were full as usual. The psychiatrist made a call on one of the patients with a pressing problem. He had committed a horrible crime. "Why did you do it?" the doctor asked. The patient declared, "God told me to." From a nearby bed a fellow sufferer loudly proclaimed, "I did not!"

The psychotic was but one of many who have claimed to be God throughout the centuries. The trouble is, everything about their lives clearly showed their claims were false. In most cases they were not only not God, they were not even normal men.

Only one Person in history has offered a valid claim to being God. He is Jesus Christ. Everything about Him—His birth, life, miraculous ministry, death, and resurrection—supports His testimony of deity. But how can God become man? He did so through the miracle of the Virgin Birth.

Luke tells the strange story of Jesus' birth in what appears to be the words of His mother, Mary. An angel announces that she is to give birth to a son. She protests that she cannot bear a child for she is a virgin. Gabriel reveals that the Holy Spirit would cause her to conceive. Thus, her child would be holy and be called the Son of God.

In faith and obedience Mary gives up the last vestige of life for self in her surrender to be the mother of Jesus. She stands to lose the love of Joseph to whom she is engaged. She risks all prospects of a happy marriage to him. Mary allows herself to be put in the most embarrassing circumstances possible; her honor, reputation, and life are at stake.

Regrettably, not everyone believes Mary's story, though it is verified with a parallel account from Joseph's point of view in Matthew. Men question it on the grounds that a virgin birth is a biological impossibility. Some suppose it is a mythological invention. Others say it is based on a misunderstanding of a prophecy in Isaiah.

Skeptics declare the account of the Virgin Birth in Luke a historical blunder, or at best a poor medical case history. In the view of some, the genealogies of Luke and Matthew show Jesus as actually Joseph's son. A few, willing to concede the possibility of the Virgin Birth, think it is so unimportant as to be unworthy of debate.

But the Christian's faith stands or falls on the truth of Mary's story. Without the Virgin Birth Jesus was not God. He may have been a good man and a great teacher, but not the Saviour. As mortal man His death at best atoned only for His own sins. The believer must answer the questions of the critics to reassure his own heart and hopefully to convince the sincere inquirer of the truth of the Virgin Birth.

A Biological Wonder

People often reject the Virgin Birth simply on the grounds that it involves the miraculous. Having rejected miracles as "unscientific" and "contrary to natural law," they declare the Virgin Birth to be impossible from a scientific point of view.

Admittedly, the Virgin Birth is a miracle. This places it outside the domain of science which formulates its descriptive natural laws after repeated observation of the facts. In other words, the logic of science is inductive, proceeding from the observation of many specific instances to the formulation of a law that covers all those instances.

Now the Virgin Birth occurred just once, hence the inductive method of science cannot be applied. So the Virgin Birth is "unscientific" only in the sense that it is outside the domain of science, not in the sense that it is impossible. If virgin births occurred often enough among humans for a scientific law to be formulated, they would no longer be miraculous. And the birth of the Son of God was important enough to demand a miracle, the Virgin Birth.

Even so, the Virgin Birth is in many ways a no greater wonder than the miracle of the original creation of Adam by God. Both the first man and the first woman were brought into the world without either father or mother (Genesis 2:7, 21, 22).

Further, virgin births are not totally unknown biologically. Parthenogenesis is the process whereby a virgin female produces young without assistance from a male. The tiny water creatures known as rotifers reproduce parthenogenetically. If they do so naturally, why is it so difficult to believe that Christ was born of a virgin supernaturally?

A Misunderstood Prophet

Some scholars protest that the Virgin Birth story is based on a misunderstanding of a prophecy in Isaiah. The prophet declares: "Behold, a virgin shall conceive, and bear a son" (Isaiah 7:14). But, some observe, Matthew does not quote directly from the Hebrew Scriptures. Instead, he quotes from the Septuagint, a third-century B.C. Greek translation of the Hebrew.

In the Septuagint, so goes this argument, the Hebrew word *almah* is incorrectly translated by the Greek word *parthenos,* which means "virgin," rather than by the Greek word *neanis* which means "young woman." In effect, this argument concludes, Matthew has carried an incorrect translation into the New Testament, referring to the young woman of Isaiah's prophecy as a virgin. It is claimed this conclusion is substantiated by Jewish failure to recognize Isaiah 7:14 as messianic.

Crucial to this objection to the Virgin Birth is the translation of the Hebrew word *almah* as "virgin." Authorities indicate it is derived from the Hebrew verb *alam* which means "to conceal" or "to hide." This concept is implicit in *almah* which means, therefore, a young woman who has not been uncovered or who has kept herself hidden from men; in other words, a virgin. Everywhere the word appears in the Old Testament this is clearly its meaning.

Hence, in both the Septuagint and in Matthew, the word is correctly translated as "virgin." That Jewish tradition does not recognize Isaiah 7:14 as messianic is irrelevant; neither does it recognize Isaiah 53 as messianic. Jewish tradition was often at cross-purposes with the Word of God (Mark 7:9, 13).

Genealogical Contradictions

Another objection to the Virgin Birth grows out of the genealogies of Jesus in Matthew and Luke. It assumes that both genealogies are Joseph's, and claims they are meaningless if Jesus was born of a virgin.

This objection assumes that because Elisabeth was of the tribe of Levi (Luke 1:5), Mary, who was her cousin (v. 36), must have been of the tribe of Levi also. Thus she was not of the tribe of Judah from which the Messiah was to come.

However, the cousinly relationship may have resulted from their mothers being sisters. Elisabeth's mother may have married a Levite, and Mary's mother may have married a member of the family of David. If this is the case, then one of the genealogies may be that of Mary. Which one? Probably Luke's, since the birth story in Luke focuses on Mary's part in it, just as Matthew's genealogy is probably Joseph's since the birth story there focuses on Joseph.

Why two genealogies? Luke's genealogy establishes the fact that Jesus is biologically a descendant of David through Mary. Significantly, Matthew 1:16 offers confirmation that Jesus was not the son of Joseph: "Jacob begat Joseph the husband of Mary, of whom was born Jesus, who is called Christ." The word *whom* in the Greek text is feminine, and refers to Mary. The change from the active verb *begat* to the passive *was born* in attributing the birth solely to Mary indicates clearly that Joseph played no part in the conception of Jesus.

This fact is confirmed by verses 24 and 25: "Joseph . . . knew her not till she had brought forth her firstborn son." Joseph's genealogy contained in Matthew, therefore, is the legal genealogy that establishes Jesus' right to the throne as the adopted son of Joseph. It does not mean Jesus was not virgin-born.

Historical Blunders

Still other critics of the doctrine of the Virgin Birth have attacked the historical accuracy of Luke 2. First they attack Luke's mention of the census. They observe that his words, "This first enrollment" (v. 2, literal translation), imply there was a series of such enrollments. They refuse to believe there was any such series, claiming there is no historical evidence to support Luke's statements. But it has now been proven that Luke was right.

Since the beginning of this century, archaeological evidence has been discovered that supports Luke's statements. The enrollment Luke describes was actually the first of a series held every 14 years. The enrollment of Acts 5:37 took place in 6 A.D., indicating that Caesar Augustus decreed the first enrollment should begin in 8 B. C. Local conditions probably prevented immediate implementation in Palestine, delaying it to 4 or 5 B. C. when Jesus was born. (The year of Jesus' birth was incorrectly calculated by a Roman monk in the sixth century, resulting in our present calendar error.)

Second, the critics charge it is ridiculous to believe people would have to go to their native villages to enroll for the census by households. But again the evidence proves Luke is right. The governor of Egypt, G. Vivius Maximus, issued an edict for the A.D. 104 census of the series. It reads: "The enrollment by household being at hand, it is necessary to notify all who for any cause are outside their homes to return to their domestic hearths. . . ."

Finally, critics charge Luke blundered in making the statement: "Cyrenius was governor of Syria" (Luke 2:2). They point out that Cyrenius was governor during the enrollment mentioned in Acts 5:37

which occurred in 6 A.D. Hence, they argue, Luke is dating the rule of Cyrenius about 10 years too early.

Again Luke has been proven historically accurate. Evidence has been discovered that proves Cyrenius was governor of Syria twice. An inscription was discovered in Rome in 1828 indicating that fact. Further, Ramsay discovered two monuments in Asia Minor that indicate Cyrenius was governor of Syria during the period in which Caesar Augustus ordered the first census, the period in which Christ was born.

The Doctor's Opinion

Critics also reject the Virgin Birth story in Luke as a poor medical case history. Paul calls Luke "the beloved physician" (Colossians 4:14). As a doctor, Luke was aware of how conception and reproduction normally take place. Yet despite his knowledge, he risked his reputation as a doctor, a man of medical science, to state that Jesus was born of Mary who was a virgin. He talked personally to Mary about the matter and believed all happened as she declared it.

Does It Really Matter?

A few, willing to concede the possibility of the Virgin Birth as a miracle, think it so unimportant as to be unworthy of debate. They admit it may be true, but ask, "Is it really important?" They point out that in the New Testament, only Matthew and Luke explicitly refer to the Virgin Birth and only in the first 2 chapters of their Books.

While it is true that explicit references to the Virgin Birth are confined to the first 2 chapters of the Gospels of Matthew and Luke in the New Testament, implicit references are found elsewhere. For example, the concept of the Virgin Birth is implicit in Christ's claim to be both David's son and David's Lord (Mark 12:35-37), a claim that becomes understandable in the light of His miraculous birth. It is implicit also in John's Gospel: "And the Word was made flesh, and dwelt among us" (John 1:14). The Virgin Birth offers an explanation of how the Word became flesh.

The Virgin Birth is important. The integrity of the Bible as the inerrant Word of God is at stake in the issue. If we are to trust the Bible elsewhere, we must be able to trust it when it refers to the Virgin Birth.

Conclusive Evidence

The story of the Virgin Birth in the New Testament rests solidly on a foundation built elsewhere. Evidence in the Old Testament is supportive of the doctrine. The testimony of the Early Church fathers in post-New Testament days indicates the acceptance of the teaching in the Church.

Evidence for the Virgin Birth in the Old Testament begins with the first promise of man's Redeemer. To Eve, God said He was to be "thy seed," with strong implications that a male would play no part in His birth (Genesis 3:15). Perhaps with this in mind, Paul declares Jesus to be "made of a woman" (Galatians 4:4). It is fitting that since sin came into the world by woman, so should the Saviour.

Isaiah declares His name will be Immanuel, "God with us" (Isaiah 7:14; cf. Matthew 1:23). Through the Virgin Birth God came to dwell with men in human form in the person of Jesus.

Micah declares that the Baby born in Bethlehem would be a "ruler in Israel; whose goings forth have been from of old, from everlasting" (Micah 5:2). Such a Child would have to be the eternal God.

Among evidence of acceptance of the Virgin Birth by the Early Church is the Apostles' Creed. The document dates back to at least 140 A.D. It refers to Jesus as One "who was conceived by the Holy Ghost, [and] born of the Virgin Mary."

The writings of the Early Church fathers have similar references. Irenaeus and Tertullian both declare that the doctrine of the Virgin Birth was well established in the Church in their day. Justyn Martyr likewise indicates the fundamental importance of the teaching in the primitive Church. Ignatius shows the doctrine was accepted among early Christians without controversy. The testimony of such men, living only one step away from the apostolic period, demands the serious attention of sincere seekers after the truth.

The doctrine of the Virgin Birth has its roots in the Old Testament. The account of the miracle is in the New Testament. Early Church fathers show its acceptance without question in the infant Church. With such conclusive evidence of its truthfulness, let the story stand!

8   Can You Believe It?

Matthew 28:1-17

Faith's Only Foundation

A missionary couple took a sight-seeing tour in a Latin American country. They visited a Catholic cathedral where there was a statue of Christ hanging on a cross. Later they visited an old Spanish mission where there was a wax figure of Christ enclosed in a glass casket. During family devotions that evening, one of the children said, "Daddy, I have seen Jesus dead so many times today. Please tell me again the story of the Resurrection. That's the best story in the whole world."

The account of Jesus' resurrection is more than just a good story. The empty tomb of Jesus was not arranged just for the sake of an argument. The doctrine of the Resurrection is a vital, life-giving one. It is faith's only foundation.

The resurrection of Christ demonstrated His deity. In Paul's words, Jesus was "declared to be the Son of God with power, . . . by the resurrection from the dead" (Romans 1:4). It also assures the believer of his salvation, for the apostle says further that Christ "was delivered for our offenses, and was raised again for our justification" (4:25). Too, it guarantees the Christian a personal bodily resurrection (1 Corinthians 15:20-23).

In fact, without the resurrection of Christ the believer woud have nothing but a false hope. In elaborating on the matter, Paul says that if Jesus did not rise from the grave, apostolic preaching is vain because the apostles would be false witnesses (vv. 12-19). Then, of course, the Christian's faith is vain, he is yet in his sins, and he is to be pitied above all men. Also, the dead in Christ have perished, if Christ did not rise.

Perhaps the crucial nature of the resurrection of Jesus explains why critics have made it the focal point for attacks on Christianity. Some say the story of the Resurrection is a fallacy because Christ didn't really die on the cross. Others declare the tomb was not actually empty, or if so it was never occupied in the first place. An old false account from New Testament days is that the body of Jesus was stolen from the grave. A few claim the appearances of the resurrected Saviour were but hallucinations, or at best mere visions.

But none of these views sufficiently explains the facts of the case. Close scrutiny of the evidence requires one to accept the simple declaration: "He is not here: for he is risen" (Matthew 28:6).

On Faking Death

Instead of actually dying, did Jesus merely "swoon" on the cross? This is the proposal of some opponents of the Resurrection story. Jesus did not really die, but being mistaken for dead, He was taken down by His friends and buried. Later He revived, perhaps as a consequence of the spices being placed in the burial garments and the laying of the body in the cool cave-tomb. Subsequently, Jesus escaped from the grave, appeared to His disciples, and then went into hiding.

But all of this is highly unlikely for several reasons.

The soldiers concluded Jesus was dead (John 19:33). The blood and water that flowed from His pierced side removed all doubt in their minds. It meant that the red corpuscles had already separated from the white serum of the blood. The centurion officially declared the execution order carried out (Mark 15:44, 45). On his testimony, Pilate ruled Jesus dead and released His body for burial.

As they prepared the body for burial, Joseph and Nicodemus would have detected life if Jesus had not been dead. The women who watched Him die at close range would have protested the burial if any hope remained that He was still alive.

Mark shows that Jesus was really dead by his choice of Greek words in telling the story. The use of the Greek word meaning *corpse* in Mark 15:45 as opposed to a different word in the Greek for *body* in verse 43 attests to the fact that Jesus was actually dead.

Jesus' own actions disprove the "swoon" theory. How could a half-dead man escape from a sealed and guarded tomb? Could He walk for a considerable distance with a weakened, mutilated body? What man in such a condition could appear to his followers as alive and unharmed by his experiences in crucifixion? To end all debate as to whether or not Jesus actually died on the cross, one need but observe that Christ himself declared He was dead (Revelation 1:18).

The Unknown Tomb

Other critics of the Resurrection story say Christ's body was never actually in the tomb visited by His followers. The objection takes two forms. Some suggest the body of Jesus was never properly buried.

Rather, it was tossed into a pit with the bodies of the criminals executed with Him that day.

Yet, all four Gospels record the burial of Jesus in a tomb. This is in accord with Deuteronomy 21:22, 23 which requires the burial of criminals on the day they are executed. The Jews who buried Jesus followed this law to the letter. The Romans frequently left such bodies on their crosses indefinitely as a warning to other criminals.

Others believe the women as well as Peter and John visited the wrong tomb. This was due to the semidarkness of the early morning hour and the confusion of the emotional stress all were under at the time.

However, such a mistake would be possible only if the place were a public cemetery. Jesus was buried in a private tomb in the garden of Joseph of Arimathea (Matthew 27:59, 60). Furthermore, Mark notes that "Mary Magdalene and Mary the mother of Joses beheld where he was laid" (Mark 15:47). Their careful marking of the spot assured no mistakes in locating the tomb as soon as the Sabbath had passed.

Even if the women had blundered as to the site of the burial, Joseph would have corrected the matter immediately. Also, in that case the enemies of Jesus would have obliged and stopped the Resurrection tale by pointing to the right tomb with the body still there.

Grave Robbers

Among early efforts to quiet the news of Jesus' resurrection was the claim that the body was stolen from the tomb. The false account was concocted by the priests and the soldiers (Matthew 28:11-15). Through a bribed agreement the guards said the body was removed while they slept. But how can the testimony of one who is asleep be valid? If true, why weren't the soldiers tried for sleeping on duty?

The fact is the disciples did not remove the body; for when they were told the tomb was empty, they disbelieved (Luke 24:9-11). The Jewish leaders and the Romans did not remove the body, for if they had they could have produced it and refuted the claims of the Resurrection. Grave robbers did not remove the body, for the linen clothes were left behind (John 20:5). Joseph of Arimathea could not have removed the body, for the soldiers had "made the sepulchre sure, sealing the stone, and setting a watch" (Matthew 27:66).

Wild Imaginations

Other attempts to discredit the Resurrection story charge the disciples with self-deception. The apostles wanted so badly to believe Old Testament prophecies of the resurrection of Jesus that they convinced themselves it happened when it didn't. Yet, John explains their hesitation to accept early Resurrection reports, saying: "For as yet they knew not the Scripture, that he must rise again from the dead" (John 20:9).

This objection further assumes the grief-stricken women were so distraught they deceived themselves into believing they saw an empty tomb. Perhaps they even hallucinated in the process.

But hallucinations are usually the experience of individuals, not groups. Jesus appeared to several groups, including one of over 500 in number (1 Corinthians 15:6). Besides, hallucinations generally are of short duration. The Bible says Jesus "showed himself alive after his passion by many infallible proofs, being seen of them forty days" (Acts 1:3).

Some agree that the post-Resurrection appearances of Jesus might have been God-produced. Even so, they say the resurrection of Jesus was spiritual rather than physical. God gave the grief-stricken disciples visions of Jesus to dull the edge of their sorrow.

If Jesus' resurrection was not physical, what happened to His body? Jehovah's Witnesses say perhaps it dissolved into gases. But to say this could happen in 3 days requires a wilder imagination than to believe in the possibility of the Resurrection.

None merely imagined seeing the risen Lord. Jesus himself indicated His resurrection was physical. He said: "Behold my hands and my feet, that it is I myself: handle me, and see; for a spirit hath not flesh and bones, as ye see me have" (Luke 24:39). Then, to prove it He ate with them. A week later He invited Thomas to touch His body (John 20:27).

Ample Evidence

The New Testament says that between the Resurrection and the Ascension Jesus appeared to His followers no less than 11 times. Seven of these were in the Jerusalem area. The others were in Galilee.

In Jerusalem He met with individuals such as Mary Magdalene (Mark 16:9) and Peter (Luke 24:34). There He also appeared to small groups, including the Emmaus two (Mark 16:12) and a band of women (Matthew 28:9). Twice before He left the holy city He made himself known in resurrection form to the apostles (John 20:20, 26).

Prior to His death Jesus made an appointment to meet with the Twelve in Galilee after His resurrection (Mark 14:28). There He met them on a mountainside (Matthew 28:16, 17) and on the seashore (John 21:1-23). While in the area He also appeared to individuals like James (1 Corinthians 15:7) and to the crowd of over 500 (v. 6).

Jesus returned to the Jerusalem area for a final meeting with His followers before the Ascension (Luke 24:50, 51). This occurred just 10 days prior to the descent of the Holy Spirit at Pentecost (Acts 1:4-11).

Admissible Testimony

How trustworthy is the testimony of these witnesses of the post-Resurrection appearances of Jesus? Generally, three things are required for a valid testimony in court. First, the person must have firsthand knowledge of the events discussed. He must be an eyewitness. Second, his character must be such that the jury can trust his testimony. Lawyers frequently discredit what witnesses of questionable character say on the stand. Third, there must be agreement among the testimonies of the various witnesses. Contradictory testimonies rarely convict the accused.

The testimonies of the post-Resurrection appearances of Jesus come from eyewitnesses. Theirs were no mere repeating the reports of others. They told what they had seen for themselves.

As to the character and honesty of the witnesses of the Resurrection, not even the severest critics question their sincerity or ethics. Their reputation stands in the court of time like that of all upright men.

True, some charge that their motives were such as to result in self-deception, but they still acknowledge that the disciples really believed what they said about the Resurrection. What other conclusion can one reach when he observes that they risked their lives to report Jesus' resurrection? Rarely is a person willing to die for what he knows to be a lie.

There is full agreement in the testimonies of the witnesses of the Resurrection. Yet, the agreement is not that of witnesses who have fabricated a story that each memorizes to recite on the witness stand. The individual accounts both project the central truth of the Resurrection and convey the absence of collaboration among the witnesses.

Cause and Effect

Not the least of the proofs of Christ's resurrection concerns cause and effect. What a difference the Resurrection made in the lives of the followers of Jesus! Their hopes of an immediate earthly kingdom with Christ as its head were dashed to pieces with His crucifixion. They were confused. They hid themselves in fear. Later they fled the Jerusalem area and thought to return to their old way of life in Galilee.

It appeared they had given all and had lost all. They were in no mood to fabricate false stories to get themselves out of a dilemma. Nothing short of positive proof that Jesus was still alive would have changed all this. That the Church survived and continues strong worldwide to this day stems from the fact of the Resurrection.

The effects of the Resurrection are most obvious in the life of Peter. His original conversion was genuine (Matthew 16:13-17). Yet, Jesus later spoke of another "conversion" that must come in Peter's life (Luke 22:31, 32). At the time Peter looked for the immediate earthly kingdom. When his hopes vanished at the cross, he went through a crisis experience which was necessary to complete his conversion. That "conversion" took place in Peter's meeting with the risen Lord.

A similar thing happened to James, a brother of Jesus. James did not believe Jesus was the Messiah during most of His ministry (John 7:5). Yet James was in the Upper Room with the others who waited for the descent of the Holy Spirit (Acts 1:14). He became a prominent leader in the Early Church (15:13; Galatians 1:19). No doubt the Resurrection made the difference with James.

A Reasonable Resurrection

Logic alone argues for the resurrection of Jesus. It is not reasonable that the life of such a Person as Christ should end in death at the hands of His enemies. This would show wrong and evil as triumphant over right and good. It would also present mankind with the problem of a Man who was truthful and wise in everything He said, except in predicting His own resurrection. Such cannot be. He was correct in promising to rise from the dead, as in everything else He spoke.

With the Resurrection so central to the gospel, it is not surprising that it provided the theme for most of the sermons in the Book of Acts. Strong suggests that if one wishes to validate the miracles of the Bible he should start with Jesus' resurrection, not with Jonah and the whale or Balaam's ass that talked.

9 Divine Parenthood

Romans 8:14-23

A Beggar's Inheritance

In one of Dr. J. Wilbur Chapman's meetings a man arose and gave the following testimony: "I got off at the Pennsylvania depot as a tramp, and for a year I begged on the streets for a living. One day I touched a man on the shoulder and said, 'Mister, please give me a dime.' As soon as I saw his face, I recognized my father. 'Father, don't you know me?' I asked. Throwing his arms around me, he cried, 'I have found you; all that I have is yours!' "

The gentleman continued: "Men, think of it, that I, a tramp stood begging my father for 10¢, when for 18 years he had been looking for me to give me all he was worth!"

In a similar way the Heavenly Father is seeking for lost sinners. He wants to bestow on the repentant sinner the unsearchable riches of Christ.

Does this mean all men are sons of God with inherent rights to a heavenly treasure? People hold various views on the subject of the fatherhood of God. In the practical realm, some say God is the Father of no one, and others say He is the Father of everyone. In a more theological realm there are those who question that God was even the Father of Jesus, while others declare that Jesus was the Father. A search of Scripture is necessary to clarify the issues.

A Father Without Children

The reason some give for saying God is not a Father is that He is not a Person. Therefore He is without children. As indicated in earlier discussion, these include the adherents of Christian Science, Unity, and Theosophy. Each group views God as some kind of impersonal principle rather than as a Person.

For Christian Science, God is the divine principle of love. Those of Unity see Him as the life principle of the universe. To adherents of Theosophy, God is the everywhere-present, impersonal World Soul.

It is true that God is love, but He is more. He is a loving Person, a Heavenly Father (Matthew 5:48). God does give life to all, but He gives abundant life only through His Son (John 10:10). God is supremely intelligent, but more, He is an intelligent Father who knows how to take care of the needs of His children (Matthew 6:8). God is everywhere present, but as a Person who is concerned for the needs of all mankind (Acts 14:17).

Schools of thought that reduce God to an impersonal principle lose the fatherhood of God in the process. The end result is a God who is far less than the God of the Bible.

A Father of Millions

At the other extreme are those who hold that God is everyone's Father. The doctrine of the universal fatherhood of God stresses that all men owe their existence to God because of His creatorship. God, the Creator-Father, loves all men, even those who are His disobedient children. Because of His fatherly love, God will eventually restore all men to fellowship with Him. This view is characteristic of universalism and modernistic liberalism.

Adolf von Harnack has provided modernists with a concise statement of their erroneous views of man (*What Is Christianity?* [NY: G. P. Putnam's Sons, 1904], trans. by Thomas Bailey Saunders). He says that the fact Jesus instructed men to address God as Father in the Lord's Prayer shows they are His children. That Jesus told men to rejoice over their names being written in heaven suggests they are safe in God for time and eternity. They cannot suffer evil either in life or in death. The Master taught this by showing that God is attentive to the death of even a sparrow. His teaching that the soul is more valuable than the whole world provides a basis for a reverence of humanity which nothing short of recognizing God as the Father of all could ever do.

A variant of the universalistic teaching appears even among fundamentalist groups. It goes under various labels, including final restitution, reconciliation of all things, and ultimate victory.

The doctrine is based on a fragment of Acts 3:21, taken out of context: "the times of restitution of all things." From this some teach the wicked will be confined to the lake of fire for a long time, during which they will be purified. At the supposed time of "final restitution," the inhabitants of the lake of fire, then completely cleansed, will be reconciled to God. Even Satan and his wicked angels will be included.

The Fate of the Rebellious

God manifests love when He pardons a repentant sinner, but His justice is shown in punishing the rebellious. The phrase "the times of restitution of all things" does not refer to Satan, the wicked angels, and wicked men who willfully rebel against God. The context shows it deals only with those who listen to that "Prophet," Christ.

The Bible teaches that the duration of punishment in the lake of fire is as long as the duration of eternal life. In Matthew 25:46 the same Greek word is translated two ways, "everlasting" and "eternal." "And these shall go away into everlasting [or, eternal] punishment: but the righteous into life eternal [or, everlasting]." One cannot say eternal life is unending and at the same time say eternal punishment will have an end.

Arguing for a final restitution of all ignores a basic teaching of Jesus. He said: "Whosoever speaketh against the Holy Ghost, it shall not be forgiven him, neither in this world, neither in the world to come" (12:32). If even one person will not be forgiven, then all are not reconciled to God. The inadequacy of the Creator-Father relationship as a basis of redemption is evident.

The Way of the Redeemed

True, in a sense, God as a creator is Father of all mankind, for He "hath made of one blood all nations of men for to dwell on all the face of the earth" (Acts 17:26). "God created man in his own image" (Genesis 1:27), making man a person. Thus, in a sense, every person, just because he is a person, witnesses to the fact of God as Father of all men.

Yet in every person, the likeness of God is blurred by sin. Paul declares: "For all have sinned, and come short of the glory of God" (Romans 3:23). Sin mars God's image in man and makes it faulty.

Sin transposes man from the place where God is his Father to the place where Satan becomes his father. Jesus told sinners who stood before Him: "Ye do the deeds of your father. . . . Ye are of your father the devil" (John 8:41, 44). The sinner is no longer a child of God. He is a child of the devil.

Of course, God does sustain a fatherly kind of relationship to all men because of His creatorship. He even loves those who have rebelled against Him and become His enemies. Paul writes: "God commendeth his love toward us, in that, while we were yet sinners, Christ died for us" (Romans 5:8).

But God becomes man's spiritual Father only through the redemption He provided in Jesus. Man, having broken the relationship to God as Father by creation, can enter into a new relationship with Him as Father only by redemption.

Then it is either redemption or punishment. The choice is man's. However, God has taken the initiative in the matter.

An evangelist was ministering in a large auditorium in Chicago. A little boy became lost in the meeting. He was brought to the platform and presented to the evangelist. The preacher took the lad in his arms and said to the crowd: "The father of this child is more anxious to find the boy than the boy is to be found. It is just so with our Heavenly Father." Interestingly, the evangelist's text that evening was Luke 19:10: "For the Son of man is come to seek and to save that which was lost."

A Fatherless Son

In a more theological realm, those who declare that God was not the Father of Jesus include the Unitarians and the Jehovah's Witnesses. As seen earlier, they believe there is only one Person in the

Godhead, the Father. To them Jesus has no deity. He is not God. In this position, overemphasis on the unity of God results in the denial of the Trinity.

The Father is God, but so is Jesus Christ, and so is the Holy Spirit. Concerning the deity of Jesus, the Bible says that "in him dwelleth all the fullness of the Godhead bodily" (Colossians 2:9). Both Jesus and the Holy Spirit are included with God the Father in the benediction of 2 Corinthians 13:14. Both are also with the Father in the formula for baptism in Matthew 28:19. Jesus told His followers: "Go ye therefore, and teach all nations, baptizing them in the name of the Father, and of the Son, and of the Holy Ghost." To say that only the Father is God is to ignore the teachings of the Bible.

The Son as Father

Among the first to teach that Jesus was both Father and Son was Sabellius in about 200 A.D. He taught a trinity of manifestations of the forms of God rather than of essence. God was manifested as the Father in the Old Testament, as the Son in the early New Testament, and as the Holy Spirit after Pentecost. There are not three Persons in the Godhead, but three manifestations of one Person.

Sabellius' views may be illustrated by the relationship a man has with himself and others as a son, a brother, and a father. He is all three, yet one person. The Church of Sabellius' day rightly rejected his teachings.

To say that God has simply manifested himself in three ways, at different times as Father, Son, and Holy Spirit, is to make Him a deceiver, if indeed He does not exist as such. If He seeks to make himself appear to be what He is not, He is neither true to

84

himself nor His creatures. The Trinity must exist in nature for there to be truth in its manifestations. For Sabellius to declare that when God says, "Thou art my beloved Son" (Luke 3:22), He is speaking to himself is nonsense.

The 20th century has produced a revival of Sabellius' old heresy. It appears among some fundamentalist groups under the names Oneness, New Issue, and Jesus Only. In this modern version of the old heresy, it is believed the name of the Person who manifests himself as Father, Son, and Holy Spirit is Jesus.

But Jesus is not the name of the Father, Son, and Holy Spirit collectively. The angel said of Mary: "She shall bring forth a son, and thou shalt call his name Jesus: for he shall save his people from their sins" (Matthew 1:21). Obviously, this was a personal name for the Man from Nazareth.

Jesus distinguished himself from the Father. He said: "I must be about my Father's business" (Luke 2:49).

The distinction is also clearly evident at the baptism of Jesus. As the Holy Spirit descended, the Father's voice spoke from heaven designating Jesus as His Son (Matthew 3:16, 17).

The Birth of Children

God wants to be the Father even to those who are sinners. That is why He sent His Son into the world. As a result, Peter says Christians "were not redeemed with corruptible things, as silver or gold, . . . but with the precious blood of Christ, as of a lamb without blemish and without spot" (1 Peter 1:18, 19).

Modernists, universalists, and believers in final restitution are right when they say God loves mankind and wants no one to be lost. God is "not willing that any should perish" (2 Peter 3:9). However, they err in not stressing the necessity of repentance and rebirth. God not only wills that none should perish, He also wills that "all should come to repentance."

Only by repenting and accepting Jesus as Saviour-Redeemer can a person truly experience God as his Father. He who is God's son by creation must also become His son by redemption if he wants to be saved. Only spiritual sonship counts in the end. Unredeemed sinners cannot pray, "Our Father which art in heaven."

The town drunk was surprised to hear that he could be born again. He expressed delightful shock to the Christian worker who approached him about the subject on the street. When he was told that rebirth was possible for him he said, "You don't say! I always thought I did well to be born the first time, let alone being born again."

But even the most moral of men must be born again to become a spiritual son of God. Nicodemus, a Jewish ruler and a member of the highest court of the land, the Sanhedrin, was an upright, learned man. He marveled when he was informed he must experience rebirth (John 3:1-13). Jesus explained to him that the way into the Kingdom for all men is not through natural but spiritual birth.

John leaves no doubt in the matter. Speaking of those who received Jesus as Saviour during His earthly ministry, He declares that they "were born, not of blood, nor of the will of the flesh, nor of the will of man, but of God" (1:13).

Benefits of Sonship

Paul discusses the benefits of sonship to God in writing to the Romans (Romans 8:14-23). He says genuine sons know they are children of God by His Spirit which bears witness within. They are sons by both birth and adoption. By the Spirit within they can say, "Abba, Father."

Paul further tells the Romans that true sons are led by the Spirit of God. Their conduct shows they are God's children. By the Spirit they can be like their Father in heaven, even in loving their enemies (Matthew 5:45). God allows the sun to shine on the evil as well as the good and sends rain on both the just and the unjust. In like manner, His children love all men and not just those that love them, as do the heathen. They strive to be like their Father and are not like those of whom one said: "In the beginning God made man in His image, and ever since man has been trying to make God in his image."

The apostle shows the Romans that Christians are heirs of God and joint-heirs with Christ (Romans 8:17). The future holds great prospects for them. There is a glory yet to be revealed in them.

Finally, Paul says Christians are now free, but there is yet a glorious liberty for the children of God. They are now redeemed, but the hope of the redemption of the physical body is yet future. The expectation of tomorrow is such that the whole creation "waiteth for the manifestation of the sons of God" (v. 19).

10 Unique Sonship

Philippians 2:5-11

On Becoming a Man

A missionary who had been sent to the West Indies to preach the gospel to the slaves found they were driven so hard during the long hours of their work that they were too tired to listen to his messages at night. The missionary knew the slaves would never hear the gospel unless he could go with them to the fields. So he went and sold himself to their master who put him into the work gang with them.

For the privilege of bringing the message of salvation to these men, the missionary was willing to become one of them, to suffer as they suffered, to live as they lived. What a picture of what Jesus did for man when He "took upon him the form of a servant, and was made in the likeness of men!" (Philippians 2:7).

Yet, in spite of the beauty of the story of the Incarnation, how God could become man remains a mystery to the finite mind of men. Focusing on this wonderous miracle, Paul exclaims: "And without controversy great is the mystery of godliness: God was manifest in the flesh" (1 Timothy 3:16).

To some the Incarnation is more than a mystery. It is a stumbling block. Almost from the beginning of the Christian message men have tried to remove the mystery by explaining away the miracle of the Incarnation.

Errors that have developed historically from these efforts center on the nature of Christ as the God-Man. False teachings concerning the person of Christ fit into three categories: those who deny the reality of His two natures, the human and the divine; those who question the completeness of the two natures; and those who confuse the issue of the union of the two natures.

All modern errors as to the person of Christ are but variations on these old themes. False teachers seem to have exhausted the possibilities early. Full knowledge of historical heresies in this area of Christian teaching helps to avoid the pitfalls of the past.

On the other hand, ignorance may lead to disaster. As Strong says, discovery of "new" theories on the nature of Christ that have already been declared dangerous is like the lad who uncovered a shell on a battlefield, proudly displayed it before parents who thought his new toy a marvel, and then had it explode in his face to the horror of all concerned. (See *Systematic Theology* by Augustus H. Strong [Westwood, NJ: Fleming H. Revell Co., 1907].)

An Adopted Son

Among the historical heresies that deny the reality of the human and divine natures of Christ are those of Ebionism and Docetism. Ebionism rejected teachings on the deity of Christ. He was not divine at all, but merely a man. The monotheistic view of the Jews who produced the error prevented them from believing that God could become man.

To the Ebionites, Jesus was but a mortal man until His baptism. He became the Christ, the "adopted" Son of God, at His baptism when the Holy Spirit descended upon Him, bestowing divine attributes upon Him.

But the Bible reveals that Jesus is God's "only begotten Son" (John 3:16), not His adopted Son. It shows that Jesus is "Immanuel" or "God with us" (Matthew 1:23). The baptism of Jesus was the occasion of His anointing for ministry, not the occasion of some supposed adoption.

A Nonhuman Being

Docetism, instead of questioning the deity of Christ, denies His humanity. The Greeks who developed the teaching were philosophically minded. To them all matter was evil, including the human body. Thus it was impossible that a righteous God could attach himself to an evil human body.

Some of those in Docetism taught that Christ only appeared to have a human body. In other words, He was but a phantom. Others claimed He had a real body, but it was spiritual rather than material in nature.

But the writer of the Book of Hebrews states clearly that Jesus was fully human: "Forasmuch then as the children are partakers of flesh and blood, he also himself likewise took part of the same" (2:14). To combat such teachings as that of Docetism, John wrote: "And every spirit that confesseth not that Jesus Christ is come in the flesh is not of God" (1 John 4:3).

The Created Creator

Among those who challenge the integrity and completeness of the human and divine natures of Christ are the Arians and the Apollinarians. The first of these was named after Arius, the fourth-century presbyter of Alexandria.

Arius believed there is only one Person in the Godhead, the Father. The Son, although worthy of worship, is a created being. He was the first and greatest of all created beings. In turn, it was through Him that the universe was created and is still administered to the present.

A modern variation of the Arian heresy is the doctrine of Jehovah's Witnesses. Like Arius, the Witnesses believe there is only one Person in the Godhead. They view Jesus as a created being who, prior to the Incarnation, was an angel superior to all other created beings, but was not God.

Arianism, ancient and modern, denies the Biblical teaching that in Christ "dwelleth all the fullness of the Godhead bodily" (Colossians 2:9). Although it recognizes that "the Word was with God," it does not recognize that "in the beginning was the Word, . . . and the Word was God" (John 1:1).

Association with God is not enough. The Word must be recognized as God and as eternally coexistent with the Father to uphold the teachings of the Bible. Paul writes: "For he, who had always been God by nature, did not cling to his prerogatives as God's equal, but stripped himself of all privilege by consenting to be a slave by nature and being born as mortal man" (Philippians 2:6, 7; *Phillips*). Jesus was and is God.

Arianism errs in its estimation of the deity of Christ. Therefore its teachings were rejected by the Council of Nicaea in 325 A.D.

A Mind of His Own

Questioning the integrity of Christ's human nature, Apollinarians declared that Jesus did not have a mind of His own. Led by Apollinaris, the fourth-century bishop of Laodicea, they taught Christ had a human body and a human soul but not a human mind or spirit. The rational spirit or mind was supplied to Jesus by the divine Logos or Word. Thus the eternal Word was united with an irrational human body. Thus, Christ was a mixture of God and man, but was neither completely God nor completely man.

In contrast to these views, Philippians 2:7 indicates that Jesus was truly human by nature. Yet, Matthew 1:23 and 1 Timothy 3:16 indicate that Jesus retained His essential deity. Jesus is the God-Man, truly God and truly man. Small wonder, then, that the Apollinarian doctrine was condemned by the Council of Constantinople in 381 A.D.

Two Persons in One

The historical heresies that confuse the issue of the union of the two natures of Christ include those of the Nestorians and the Eutychians. The first of these arose from the teachings of Nestorius, a fifth-century patriarch of Constantinople.

Nestorius reacted against the teachings of Apollinaris. Instead of Jesus being neither completely God nor completely man, He had two very distinct natures, the human and the divine. These two natures remained separate throughout His life. They functioned harmoniously, but never united.

Nestorius viewed the divine nature of Christ operating in Him somewhat like the indwelling Spirit functions in any believer. The basic difference was in the unlimited supply and the absolute control of the Spirit which Jesus experienced. In the ordinary Christian the supply is not infinite, nor is the control complete at all times.

The Nestorians also illustrated the union of the two natures of Christ by referring to marriage. Two individuals become one in matrimony, but always remain two distinct persons.

The particular stress Nestorius placed on the distinction between the two natures made it almost impossible to think of Jesus as one Person. Instead of a genuine organic union of the human and the divine in Christ, Nestorius seemed to teach a moral union of the two natures. To teach that their separate wills cooperated harmoniously did not solve the problem.

The Bible indicates that Jesus was and is one Person. He always referred to himself in the singular, not the plural. God was not only manifested in the flesh (1 Timothy 3:16), He also became flesh (John 1:14). Jesus had two natures, but He was one Person with a single will. He said: "For I came down from heaven, not to do mine own will, but the will of him that sent me" (6:38).

Because of his false views of Christ, Nestorius was dismissed as the patriarch of Constantinople in 431.

Superstar

Another way of confusing the issue as to the union of the two natures in Christ is to say they combined to produce someone who was neither human nor divine. This, in essence, is what Eutyches taught in the early part of the fifth century.

Eutychians believed that the divine united with the human in Christ much as a drop of honey mixes with water in a glass. The nature of both changes so that one no longer has either honey or water, but a unique third element.

The danger of this view is that it makes Jesus superhuman. It virtually declares that even His body was divine. But if He were not fully human, then He could not provide a human sacrifice for man's sins.

Eutychianism also robs Jesus of His deity. It makes Him less than God. If he were not fully God then He could not serve as the perfect sacrifice for sin which the Law demands. For these reasons the teachings of Eutyches were condemned by the Council of Chalcedon in 451 A.D.

Son of Man

In contrast to the many false views of Christ, orthodox Christianity views Jesus as one Person with two natures, both human and divine. The two are complete so that He is fully God and fully man, not half God and half man. Furthermore, they are organically united, but not in such a way as to produce a third nature in the process.

Christ's humanity is symbolized by His favorite title for himself, the Son of Man. In his genealogy of the Christ, Luke is careful to show Him as the "son of Adam" (Luke 3:38).

As a man, Jesus hungered (Matthew 4:2; 21:18); thirsted (John 4:7; 19:28); became weary (4:6); needed sleep (Mark 4:38); was tempted (Luke 4:1-13; Hebrews 4:15); needed to pray (Mark 1:35); suffered (Hebrews 2:9); and died (John 19:33). All of this witnesses conclusively to His human nature.

Son of God

But if Jesus were *merely* a man, He would be a sinful man. His death, at best, then, would have availed only for His own sins. It could not have atoned for another.

However, before His birth as a man, Christ existed as God, "being in the form of God" (Philippians 2:6). He was God the Son, the Second Person of the Trinity. Calling Christ "the Word," John says: "In the beginning was the Word, and the Word was with God, and the Word was God" (John 1:1). Christ is the Word because through Him God spoke His greatest message to man.

While on earth Jesus declared himself to be God. In healing a paralytic, He first forgave the man his sins. His critics charged that only God could do that. In response, His healing word demonstrated "that the Son of man hath power on earth to forgive sins" (Mark 2:10). For repeatedly announcing that He was God, His enemies finally crucified Him.

Humiliation

In becoming man, Christ "made himself of no reputation" or "emptied himself" (Philippians 2:7). But in the emptying process, He did not empty himself of His divine nature. After He emptied himself Christ was still God. He remained God (1 Timothy 3:16).

However, Christ truly humbled himself when He took on the form of man. He voluntarily let go of His equality of position with God the Father (Philippians 2:6, 7). For one thing, His self-emptying resulted in self-imposed restrictions of knowledge. As an example, He did not know the time of the Second Coming (Mark 13:32).

Furthermore, on earth Christ did not allow himself the independent exercise of omnipotence. He said:

"The Son can do nothing of himself, but what he seeth the Father do: for what things soever he doeth, these also doeth the Son likewise" (John 5:19).

Exaltation

Because Christ emptied himself and became man in order to do the will of the Father, God has highly exalted Him (Philippians 2:9). His glory and honor have been restored. He has the position of power and authority at the Father's right hand (Ephesians 1:20).

Yet, despite His exaltation, Christ carries with Him the result of the Incarnation. He ascended into heaven with a body of flesh and bones (Luke 24:39, 51). He yet retains His human nature. Even after His ascension He is still called man. Paul writes: "For there is one God, and one mediator between God and men, the man Christ Jesus" (1 Timothy 2:5).

Nor has Christ regained His equality with the Father. He will never do so. Although the entire creation will someday be subject to the Son, the Son will be subject to the Father. Paul declares: "And when all things shall be subdued unto him, then shall the Son also himself be subject unto him that put all things under him, that God may be all in all" (1 Corinthians 15:28).

When God the Son voluntarily relinquished His equality of relation to the Father, He did it not only for time, but also for eternity. It cost Christ more to become man than most realize, yet He did so to show His great love for all men.

11   Back to the Beginning

Psalm 19:1-6

Man and the Monkey

It was his first day at school. The 6-year-old returned home full of enthusiasm. He rushed up to his dad with what appeared to be a serious question provoked by the day's academic activities.

"Dad," he said, "Do monkeys peel bananas before they eat them?" Patiently the father, who had spent time on an island in the Pacific during World War II, took time to explain the eating habits of monkeys to the lad. When he had finished, the boy simply said, "I thought if I found some old monkey somewhere he would tell me all about it!"

Though the whole matter was intended as a joke, the father, like most people, resented the implication in it that man is related to the monkey. The suggestion strikes a blow at the fundamental dignity of human beings.

Yet, many are convinced that man sprang from the monkey. Various evolutionary theories suggest this. These include the views of continuous, chance, and purposive evolution as well as the "big-bang" and "oscillating" theories of modern science. A study of these and the basic arguments for evolution in general shows that the facts used to support these positions fit better into the framework of the teachings of Scripture on special creation.

Continuous Creation

One evolutionary position is that of continuous creation. It has also been called the "steady-state theory."

According to this view, the universe remains in a more or less steady state because of the supposed continuous creation of hydrogen atoms which are believed to be the basic material out of which all matter in the universe is made.

Unlike the opinion of more recent scientists that the universe is running down, the continuous creation theory views the universe as being in a steady state and as always having been in a steady state. If hydrogen particles are continuously being created (and there is no evidence to suggest they are), and if the universe has always been in a steady state (all the evidence is to the contrary), then it follows that the universe had no beginning. From this it would follow that the Biblical statement, "In the beginning God created the heaven and the earth" (Genesis 1:1), is false because there would have been no beginning.

The leading proponent of the continuous creation theory is Professor Fred Hoyle, an English astronomer. He is an avowed atheist. However, he does not escape the necessity of God by assuming the universe had no beginning. Creation is a theological concept, not a scientific one. One must ask: "What about this supposed continuous creation process? Continuous creation by whom or what?" It seems that one actually needs the concept of a Creator to support this view.

The need for God to support the processes of the universe is obvious to those who are seeking an insight into truth. So it was with Aristotle, the pagan philosopher who lived about four centuries before Christ. After analyzing substance and movement in nature, Aristotle concluded that a First Mover or First Principle must exist. In his words: "On such a principle, then, depend the heavens and the world of nature. . . . We say therefore that God is a living being, eternal, most good, so that life and duration continuous and eternal belong to God; for this is God."

Aristotle discovered in nature exactly what the Bible indicates can be discovered about God there (Romans 1:19, 20; Acts 14:17). The Bible declares: "In the beginning God created the heaven and the earth" (Genesis 1:1), and indicates that by Christ "all things consist" or are held together (Colossians 1:17) because Christ is "upholding all things by the word of his power" (Hebrews 1:3).

Chance Evolution

A second position that some offer as a substitute for the view of special creation taught in Scripture is that of chance evolution.

Evolution is the term used to denote the supposed process by which simple things become more complex. In this view, the universe is regarded as a closed system. Everything in the universe is a product of development within the system rather than a result of a creative supernatural intrusion into the system from without. Thus, as its title implies, this theory proposes that the universe developed by chance, life developed by chance, and man developed by chance.

However, chance evolution leaves unanswered the origin of the basic substance from which life is supposed to have evolved. It is no easier to believe in an eternal substance than to believe in the eternal God. Besides, if the universe came into being by chance, couldn't it cease to exist by the same way? The future under such a philosophy is bleak indeed.

Out of a Bang

What might be considered a variation of the chance theory of evolution is the "big-bang" hypothesis. Due more to the operation of natural laws than chance, the theory holds that the universe had a definite beginning and it will have an end.

Big-bang theorists speculate that in the beginning the universe was confined to a highly compact, relatively small, and extremely hot concentration of matter. A gigantic explosion projected particles from the center of the universe to begin the formation of galaxies. These continue to disperse leaving blank spaces in the universe. The galaxies with their systems of stars continuously burn up the basic hydrogen of the universe. Once the hydrogen is all gone, the galaxies will fade away, and the universe will cease to be.

But questions left unanswered here include: "Where did the primordial hydrogen come from originally? What caused the big bang that started the formation of the universe? What conditions existed before the big bang?"

An Oscillating Universe

To counteract the morbid view that all things are running down, other chance evolutionists propose an oscillating theory of the universe. In their view the universe is in an endless cycle of expansion and contraction. At present it is in an expansion phase which began when matter was subjected to its highest possible degree of concentration. As the expansion cycle gradually runs down, eventually it will reverse itself into the concentration phase again. Once that is complete and expansion begins again, the universe is born anew, and so on for eternity.

The oscillating theory of evolution seems to correspond to the Eastern philosophy of an unending cycle of birth, life, death, and rebirth. Such runs counter to the Christian view that all things will consummate in a better world according to God's perfect plan for the ages.

Purposive Evolution

Many evolutionists recognize that chance is insufficient to account for the supposed evolutionary process. Hence they assume the existence of a purpose either inside or outside of nature which gave direction to the development of the universe and everything in it. Since there is no purpose without someone to have a purpose, some evolutionists assume God guided the process by which one form is supposed to have evolved from another.

Since evolutionism believes that one form of life developed from another, the forms of life would have to be continuous, one form of life leading smoothly into another form. But there is no scientific evidence to support the belief that transitional forms either exist or ever have existed. Scientists are at a loss to explain the gaps existing between the various forms of life. Clearly, then, evolutionism, even that which admits the existence of God, is inadequate to account for life as it exists.

Evolving Evolution

Evolution remains a philosophical concept rather than a scientific fact. The available facts that scientists have at their disposal are capable of varying interpretations. Well-known scholars such as Darwin usually have an established way of looking at life before they study available evidence. To present an orderly view of what they find, they generally interpret the facts according to their own personal philosophy.

The evolutionary concept did not originate with Charles Darwin. It was suggested long before the time of Christ by Anaximander. The theory of the development of all things from the simple to the complex was also held by Empedocles in the fifth century B.C. In the 18th century a British scientist, Buffon, declared the modification of species. A little later Lamarck propagated the idea that organisms adapted themselves to a continuously hostile environment. It seems, then, that Darwin simply adopted an existing philosophy and interpreted the evidence he found so as to support it.

Creature Classification

But the set of data that Darwin and scientists since him have at their disposal need not be interpreted in the evolutionary framework. Indeed, the facts fit better in the context of the teachings of Scripture on special creation.

One area of evidence for the evolutionists is their classification system. Since science cannot explain the gaps existing between the various forms of life, evolutionism has constructed a "family tree" of evolution. Creatures are classified on the basis of similarity of structure. The greater the degree of similarity, the greater the family relationship. Thus man and ape are classified in the same family. This, then, supposedly indicates common origin.

However, when it comes to placing items in the different categories on the basis of distinguishing characteristics, great weaknesses appear in scientific taxonomy. As to the anthropological classification of the races, for example, there are no more than a dozen or so distinguishing features, while at the same time there are a countless number of similarities. It seems wiser, then, to emphasize that man is one rather than to focus on racial differences. As Paul says: God "made of one blood all nations of men for to dwell on all the face of the earth" (Acts 17:26).

With apparent weaknesses in the evolutionary classification system, placing items in the various categories becomes almost an abitrary matter. Thus, the system does not seem to constitute valid evidence for the evolutionary concept. A British zoologist, Dr. E. L. G. Watson, says: "The vast body of the tree of evolution is entirely imaginary."

Comparing Bodies

Closely related to the scientific classification system is another area frequently used as evidence in support of evolution. It is that of comparative anatomy.

In comparing the bodies of animals, for example, similarity of bone structure is said to indicate common ancestry. This is generally demonstrated in a comparison of the cat and horse foreleg with the human arm.

However, couldn't similarity of bone structure

speak more of a Common Designer than of a common ancestor? Designers of buildings, great artists, and famous musicians carry enough of what they have used in one project to another project so that men come to recognize their work wherever it appears.

Fetal Development

Another area of evolutionary evidence is known as the recapitulation theory or the biogenetic law. It states that during the embryonic development of the human fetus the organism passes through all the evolutionary stages of historical man. Thus in 9 months it traces the steps of its primitive ancestors through the centuries.

However, reputable scientists of the present no longer appeal to this area of evidence for evolution. As an example of the reasons for this, at one time some marks on the human fetus were viewed as resembling the gills of the fish. These supposedly developed into the breathing apparatus of the infant. Now it is known that they have no connection with the development of the respiratory system in man.

Location Is All

Still other evidence for evolution has to do with the geographical distribution of certain species. To illustrate, the discovery of 13 "species" of finches on an isolated island caused Darwin to conclude that they all sprang from one source. He thought it unreasonable that so many different finches came into being through special creation.

But could not the facts simply indicate that God put within the original pair of finches the possibility of variety? Such, then, would argue for within-species variation, rather than across-species evolution. The first could be referred to as horizontal and the second as vertical evolution.

Selective Breeding

Another similar argument for evolution concerns the results of selective breeding. Can it not be demonstrated, for example, that through careful breeding practices one can develop a new breed of cattle? Is it not possible that all breeds of dogs came from an original pair?

Again here, though, the evidence argues for horizontal evolution, or within-species variation, and not for vertical evolution. Breeding across species, where possible at all, results in sterile offspring.

The Rock Record

A final area of evidence for evolution is the rock record. Fossils in the rocks supposedly furnish concrete evidence of the evolutionary process. It is claimed that fossils of simple plant and animal life are found in the oldest layers of rocks. The fossils of the most complex forms of life, on the other hand, appear in the youngest layers of rocks.

Actually, though, evidence contrary to evolution appears in the rocks. For one thing, fossils of more complex life appear in rocks under those with fossils of simpler life. Also, there is no evidence of transitional life forms in the rocks. If reptiles evolved into birds, where are the reptile-bird fossils?

Evolutionary Means

Among the supposed means of evolution are mutations and the tendency toward the survival of the fittest. Here again, one need not interpret the facts in an evolutionary context.

If indeed the fittest survive, why is it that 90 percent of the snakes on earth are nonpoisonous? Wouldn't the poisonous ones be the heartiest? And why are there only poisonous and nonpoisonous snakes with none in between?

As to mutation providing the means for a sudden surge from one kind or species of life to another, the evidence once more is contrary. The fact that mutations are so rare, and in most cases are harmful rather than helpful to the species, makes them a most doubtful means for evolution.

Evolution stresses continuity, the smooth flow of life from one form to another. The Bible, on the other hand, stresses discontinuity. It indicates decisive steps in creation. Six times God spoke, and six times something completely new was brought into being. Here is no gradualism of evolution; here is creative action by God.

12   The Best Teacher

Acts 22:1-16

Learning by Experience

Four people were riding on a plane together; a Roman Catholic priest, a Protestant minister, a farmer, and an atheist. The atheist asked the priest, "What is the best proof of the truth of Christianity?" The priest talked about church councils, tradition, and the like. The atheist found little interest in all that.

The atheist then asked the same question of the minister. The minister replied by discussing the authority of the Bible and the exclusive claims of Christianity. Again, though, the atheist was little attracted to what was said.

The minister then directed the atheist's attention to the farmer who was a member of his congregation. Rather amused, the atheist turned to the farmer and said, "And what can you possibly add to what the others have told me?" Enthusiastically the farmer told of his conversion experience and of what Christ meant to him in daily life. The atheist warmed to his story and was eventually converted.

Accounts of personal human experience are always appealing. Sometimes they are powerfully persuasive. Frequently when two debate a cause where the one has only an argument and the other an experience, the latter will win.

When one passes a display in a department-store window, enters, and purchases the advertised items according to the terms he read through the glass, it does little good for a friend outside to question the genuineness of the ad. The possessor of the goods learned of the truth of the offer by personal experience.

The blind man who was healed by Jesus could not match wits with the intellectuals of his day. He was not schooled in how to combat their arguments against the Master point by point. However, he could say: "One thing I know, that, whereas I was blind, now I see" (John 9:25). In his case experience was the best teacher as to who Christ was.

A Trustworthy Teacher

Still, some question whether or not experience is a trustworthy teacher. Strangely, some with a pragmatic view of life who say one learns only by experience in the realm of science, look with disdain at others who suggest that one good way to learn about religion is through experience. Why should the one be viewed as an objective study of reality while the other is seen as a subjective experience only for mystics? Why is experience considered a valid teacher in one area and not in another?

In spite of the obvious inconsistency, there are always those who scoff at the experience of the Christian. For them personal testimony does not constitute valid evidence of the genuineness of Christianity. They fall into three general classes: those who hold that religion is an appendage of an immature race; those who view the Christian as an abnormal person; and those who consider the Christian philosophy as merely a tool of adjustment for those who need such to find some semblance of order in life. An analysis of each of these positions reveals the fallacies associated with them.

Racial Immaturity

First, consider those who suggest that religion is but an appendage of an immature race. Sometimes they refer to it as "racial neurosis."

A neurosis is a minor functional nervous disorder with psychological rather than physiological origins which results in maladjustment. Sigmund Freud has called religion "the universal obsessional neurosis of humanity." By this he meant that religion is a psychological disorder that characterizes mankind as a whole.

Religion, Freud believed, was a result of man's trying to solve his problems emotionally rather than intellectually. He compared the development of the race with the development of a child. Just as a child passes through a stage of maladjustment, so the race is passing through a stage of maladjustment which it will eventually outgrow. The result will be the abandoning of religion, Freud believed.

A somewhat similar view was held by Auguste Comte. He divided the course of history into three stages. The lowest stage is the theological in which man attempts to explain reality by assuming the existence of supernatural persons. The second stage is the metaphysical in which man attempts to explain reality by abstract principles and in so doing abandons attempts to explain reality by supernatural persons. The third stage is the scientific in which man abandons all attempts to explain reality and contents himself with describing reality in measurable terms. This means that in the course of history, supernatural religion would be left behind. Instead of supernatural religion, Comte advocated a "religion of humanity," meaning an unselfish dedication to service and love.

Common to both Freud and Comte is the idea that supernatural religion is a symptom of racial immaturity, and the idea that eventually supernatural religion will be left behind by the race. Common to both is the judgment that the religious adjustment to reality is an inferior adjustment, although only Freud views it as a kind of psychological disorder.

Who Is Naive?

Have Freud and Comte and others who share their views really progressed beyond the thinking of the Christian? Or have they merely regressed to the views described by Paul as "the wisdom of the world?" Surely, the latter alternative is the true one.

Paul writes of those who mock Christianity as merely the way of the simple: "Where is the wise? where is the scribe? where is the disputer of this world? hath not God made foolish the wisdom of this world? For after that in the wisdom of God the world by wisdom knew not God, it pleased God by the foolishness of preaching to save them that believe. . . . Because the foolishness of God is wiser than men" (1 Corinthians 1:20, 21, 25).

Not that the Christian philosophy is actually a simple or naive one, for Paul goes on to say: "Howbeit we speak wisdom among them that are perfect: yet not the wisdom of this world, nor of the princes of this world, that come to nought: but we speak the wisdom of God in a mystery, even the hidden wisdom, which God ordained before the world unto our glory" (2:6, 7).

The fact is, then, any view which denies the reality of God and of His provision through Christ is regression, not progression. It is those who deny the reality of the Christian experience who are foolish, not those who have it. In contrast to the lack of understanding on the part of the natural man Paul says: "But he that is spiritual judgeth all things" (v. 15).

Personal Abnormality

Those of a second group who question the validity of Christian experience view it as a personal abnormality. To them Christianity is but a crutch for emotional cripples. Those who claim a conversion experience were duped by the mob psychology of the evangelist. They would have done better to see a psychiatrist.

Of course, persons who have experienced conversion are in the minority. In 1929 Elmer T. Clark published *The Psychology of Religious Awakening* (NY: The Macmillan Company) containing the results of his studies. Clark found that 6.7 percent of his subjects had a religious awakening of the definite crisis type, 27.2 percent of his subjects had a religious awakening that they remembered because a little emotion was involved, and 66.1 percent had a gradual awakening.

Although Clark allowed his subjects to define conversion for themselves, one thing is clear: those who experienced conversion in the sense in which evangelicals use the term were in a small minority, perhaps most of the first group and some of the second.

From the obvious fact that persons who have been converted constitute a small minority, some people conclude that the evangelical Christian conversion experience is abnormal. People forming this conclusion may think of themselves as Christian because they have religious backgrounds, religious ideals, and attend church regularly. And since they are in the majority, they think of their experience as normal and of the evangelical Christian conversion experience of the minority as abnormal. "There are more of us," they say, "therefore we must be right and you must be wrong. We have the normal Christian experience, and your experience is abnormal."

Majority Rule

However, truth is one thing that cannot be decided by a majority vote. Lowell wrote: "Truth forever on the scaffold, wrong forever on the throne" (James R. Lowell, "Poetical Works," *The Complete Writings of James Russell Lowell*, vol. 9 [Cambridge: Riverside Press, 1904]). That persons with an evangelical Christian conversion experience are in the minority should not surprise anyone. Jesus said: "Enter ye in at the strait gate: for wide is the gate, and broad is the way, that leadeth to destruction, and many there be which go in thereat: because strait is the gate, and narrow is the way, which leadeth unto life, and few there be that find it" (Matthew 7:13, 14).

The word *abnormal* as applied to the Christian ought not to frighten anyone. It simply means "deviating from the average." Did not Jesus expect

His followers to deviate from the world's standard of averageness? He declared: "They are not of the world" (John 17:16). In saying this, He meant their experience and behavior is different from the average experience and behavior of the world. In other words, it is abnormal.

Christian Psychotics

But the charge of personal abnormality against those claiming a Christian experience goes further than just that they are different, perhaps neurotically so. Some notice that psychotics in mental institutions frequently claim to be Jesus or God. Many of them declare they have sinned against the Holy Spirit. For that reason, they feel, they are in their sad condition. Many charge, therefore, that religion drives people crazy.

In a research project, Wayne Oates found no support for this common concept. In *Religious Factors and Mental Illness* (NY: Association Press, 1955) he reports that 70 percent of those he studied in a mental hospital were not religious before becoming psychotic. Another large percentage had rebelled against, instead of being loyal to, the religion of their parents.

Rather than contributing to mental illness, the gospel as taught in Scripture promotes mental health. It provides the only real solution to man's basic problem of guilt. If one has broken the law of God and senses condemnation, he can be free by repentance, confession, and faith in Christ.

In case he wrestles with false guilt after conversion, feeling he has done wrong when he knows he hasn't, the Christian has words like those of Paul to reassure him. Paul declares: "There is therefore now no condemnation to them which are in Christ Jesus" (Romans 8:1). With these words he can successfully resist the "accuser of our brethren" (Revelation 12:10).

Instrument of Adjustment

Members of a third group who reject the validity of religious experience view it as an instrument of adjustment. They concede that, to the extent religion helps a person maintain a satisfactory adjustment to life, it is good.

William James, whose *Varieties of Religious Experience* (Riverside, NJ: Macmillan Publishing Co., 1961) is a classical expression of this point of view, writes: "The religious individual tells you that the divine meets him on the basis of his personal concerns." He continues: "Religion, occupying herself with personal destinies and keeping thus in contact with the only absolute realities which we know, must necessarily play an eternal part in human history."

Does this mean James views the specifically Christian experience as one to be sought after? Not at all. Each individual must seek the kind of religious experience that enables him to adjust best to reality. James says: "Each, from his peculiar angle of observation, takes in a certain sphere of fact and trouble, which each must deal with in a unique manner . . . for each man to stay in his own experience, whate'er it be, and for others to tolerate him there, is surely best."

This view assumes that all religions are potentially of equal value, that there is no form of religious experience that is inherently better than other forms. Perhaps other religions do help people somewhat in adjusting to reality, but there is only one way of salvation. Peter said: "Neither is there salvation in any other: for there is none other name under heaven given among men, whereby we must be saved" (Acts 4:12). Jesus said: "I am the way, the truth, and the life: no man cometh unto the Father, but by me" (John 14:6).

It is true that the Christian experience helps one adjust to reality now, but more than this, it readies him for the heaven he will experience later.

Assured Christians

The person who has not been born again is handicapped in his pursuit of religious truth. Paul declares: "The natural man receiveth not the things of the Spirit of God: for they are foolishness unto him: neither can he know them, because they are spiritually discerned" (1 Corinthians 2:14). Therefore, others can place little confidence in his conclusions concerning spiritual matters. By his lack of experience concerning spiritual things, he is disqualified to speak authoritatively about them.

On the other hand, those who have been born again can speak authoritatively concerning spiritual experience. They know whereof they speak. The Spirit itself bears witness with their spirit that they are the children of God (Romans 8:15, 16). The witness of the Spirit is stronger than all the arguments the scoffers can muster. With Paul, each Christian can say: "I know whom I have believed, and am persuaded that he is able to keep that which I have committed unto him against that day" (2 Timothy 1:12).

The One and the Many

The Bible shows that an appeal to religious experience is valid. Paul related the story of his conversion to a mob in Jerusalem that moments before had stopped just short of taking his life (Acts 22:1-16). He forfeited his opportunity to defend himself in favor of a chance to witness to them.

What happens to all Christians at conversion is an equally significant experience for them. They too wish to share their story for the benefit of others. They know that when God made man in His own image, He made it possible for man to have fellowship with his Creator. Therefore man's consciousness is exposed to a spiritual environment. The soul's capacity for communion with God leaves it unsatisfied apart from such fellowship. Conversion is the beginning of fellowship with God and makes possible the other experiences that follow.

For this reason the appeal of the Christian to personal knowledge of Jesus is to more than just the one crisis experience at conversion. In addition to conversion, he has many experiences with God throughout his life.

Nor is the Christian's appeal just to a feeling when he refers to experience. What he senses in walking with God involves the whole man—his emotions, intellect, and will.

The believer knows, of course, that Christian evidences include more than human experience. His experiences must have objective reality. Christ lived in history. One can have head knowledge of Him from a Book. By experience one can know Him in the heart.

13 The Way It Is

John 18:33-38

To Tell the Truth

One's words ought to always correspond to the facts. When a 12-year-old boy was a witness in a law suit, the opposing lawyer asked, thinking to trap him, "Your father has been telling you how to testify, hasn't he?" The boy answered that he had. "Exactly how did your father tell you to testify?" asked the lawyer. "He told me to tell the truth so I would say the same thing every time," answered the boy.

To speak the truth is of prime consideration to most people. Preliminary to speaking the truth is the pursuit of truth. In this connection the words of Jesus are frequently quoted: "Ye shall know the truth, and the truth shall make you free" (John 8:32).

However, too often Jesus' words are wrested out of context by an orator, and given an application He did not mean them to have. Sometimes the so-called truth to which the orator refers is an intellectual idea; sometimes, a political theory; sometimes, a moral principle; or, sometimes, a scientific discovery.

With the term *truth* so loosely used, so freely bandied about, and so easily adapted to the purposes of the user, it is no wonder that Pilate skeptically asked, "What is truth?" (John 18:38). Is there such a thing as truth? If so, is there more than one kind of truth? If so, are all kinds of truth equally valuable? and will all kinds of truth set one free?

In a time when such a premium is placed on the notion of truth, the Christian must come to grips with what he means by truth. When the skeptic asks with Pilate, "What is truth?" the Christian must be able to respond intelligently and Biblically, for only the kind of truth referred to in the Bible will actually set one free.

Men in general tend to think in terms of three kinds of truth, perceptual truth, conceptual truth, and utilitarian truth. In a dimension beyond the ordinary, men must also give attention to intuitive and revelatory truth. This leads to a consideration of absolute, personal, moral, and liberating truth. One must study all of these to know the real truth and to come to the truth that sets men free.

Perceptual Truth

One possible way of finding truth is through direct observation. According to this approach, truth depends on the accurate perception of things as they actually are. Truth is present to the degree that an idea corresponds to, or conforms with, reality as it is. Truth must correspond with fact. A true idea about the objective world reveals something about the nature of the world. A true idea is a judgment rooted in reality.

This theory of truth is all right as far as it goes. Its weakness is that it has no necessary view of the nature of reality. Until a person knows what it considers to be real, he does not know where it will apply its essentially common-sense test of truth. And this does make a difference.

For example, suppose a person considers only the physical world to be real. He will then say he considers statements about the physical world to be true to the extent that those statements accurately reflect the nature of the physical world. As far as he has gone, one can agree with him. But he has not gone far enough, in that he has refused to admit into the arena of truth statements about the world of values, the world of persons, and the world of spirit.

Still another person may hold that it is possible to make true statements about the natural world, including values and persons, and refuse to admit the possibility of true statements about the supernatural world.

However, only when God is taken into account can one begin to speak of ultimate truth. Truth without God is partial and limited. As the ancient wise man declared: "The fear of the LORD is the beginning of knowledge" (Proverbs 1:7).

Conceptual Truth

A second way of discovering truth is through logic or reason. According to this approach, truth depends on the harmony of one idea believed to be true with another idea believed to be true. Two statements, each believed to be true, ought to be consistent. A system of true ideas ought to cohere or be congruous. A true idea is a judgment that is consistent with other true judgments. Thus, through reasoning one may discover a truth that isn't available by direct observation.

This approach to truth is also all right as far as it goes, but it has two weaknesses. First, it does not necessarily assume that the test of correspondence ought to precede the test of consistency. A moment of reflection will reveal that it is about things as they are that one ought to have consistent ideas. No amount of consistency will make up for ideas being contrary to basic facts.

The second weakness of this approach is that it may overvalue human reason. It may so stress the importance of consistency on the human level that it forgets man is finite and his ability to reason is limited.

Take the matter of divine predestination and human free will, for example. Here both weaknesses of consistency as a test of truth become apparent. The Bible teaches both predestination and free will, often in the same paragraph. For example, the death of Christ was predestined, but it involved the free actions of men (Mark 14:21; Acts 2:23).

At the finite, human level of understanding, predestination and free will seem to be inconsistent. It is difficult to understand how a thing can be predestined if it involves free will. The human tendency is to throw out either free will or pre-destination because one does not understand how both can be true. But if he does this, he sacrifices the correspondence of his ideas with the Bible's statements concerning spiritual reality because he overvalues human reason. In other words, he assumes that if he cannot understand it, God cannot either.

Does this mean one ought not to use consistency as a test of truth? Not at all. It simply means that a person ought to be more concerned about his ideas corresponding to reality than about the internal consistency of a system of ideas. One's ideas about reality should be as consistent as possible, but not falsify reality in order to achieve an artificial consistency. It is more important to accept what the Bible says is true than to understand how it can be true. Remember, God has "made foolish the wisdom of this world" (1 Corinthians 1:20).

Utilitarian Truth

Another approach to truth is concerned only with that which is functional in the present. According to this view, truth is dependent on whether an idea works or not. The consequences flowing from an idea when it is put into use test the truth of an idea. In other words, results test truthfulness.

Here again is an approach to truth that is all right as far as it goes. One should believe that something true will work if it is put into practice. For example, when James wrote: "Faith without works is dead" (James 2:20); and, "I will show thee my faith by my works" (v. 18), he was saying that faith ought to result in works, and that where there are no works, there is no true faith.

In effect, James said, "If faith, then works; if no works, then no faith." Now think for a moment. Is this the same as, "If works, then faith?" Obviously not. A person may work for many reasons, only one of them being that he has faith. He may also work because he has no faith and is trying to earn salvation.

Now the weakness of this approach to truth becomes apparent. While one can say that if something is true it will work, he cannot say that because it works it is true. To do so is to commit a logical fallacy.

Hence, this test of truth must be preceded by the other tests, namely the perceptual and conceptual tests. First, one must ask: "Does the idea correspond to or conform with reality as it actually is?" Then: "Is the idea consistent with other ideas believed to be true?" And finally: "Does it work?"

All these approaches to truth, then, are necessary to test the truthfulness of an idea. But they come short in leading one to the whole truth. Certainly perceptual, conceptual, and utilitarian truth do not constitute the whole truth, for they do not include the all-important areas of intuitive and revelatory truth.

Absolute Truth

The problem is the approaches to truth discussed so far are limited by finiteness. Perceptual truth is limited by how accurately one perceives reality and how well he puts it into ideas. Conceptual truth is limited by one's ability to achieve consistency on the finite level of human understanding. Utilitarian truth is limited by the ability to see cause-effect relationships.

All of these have their values. The truthfulness of ideas and the truthfulness of statements communicating ideas is important, make no mistake about that. Jesus said: "If it were not so, I would have told you" (John 14:2); indicating that He is concerned about this kind of truth.

Yet beyond this kind of truth there is absolute truth, in other words, *the* truth. Jesus said: "I am ... the truth" (v. 6). Jesus is the Absolute Truth compared to which all other truth is limited and partial. Anything else that is reported to be true must be measured against Jesus who is the Truth.

Personal Truth

Notice that Jesus is a Person. This means the truth of which He spoke is personal truth. Words, sentences, prepositions—these are limited in their ability to convey the nature of ultimate reality. Why? Because ultimate reality is a Person, God. God spoke to man "word-wise" through the prophets, but His ultimate word to man is the Son, the Word.

Notice how the Weymouth translation of Hebrews 1:1, 2, puts it: "God, who of old spoke to our fore-fathers in many fragments and by various methods through the Prophets, has at the end of these days spoken to us through a Son." That says it very well. The fragmentary, piecemeal revelation given through the prophets has been summed up once for all in a Person, God's Son. Jesus is the center and ultimate expression of all truth as the revelation of the Father.

Moral Truth

It is because truth is ultimately personal that it is moral. There is more to truth than mere point-for-point agreement between words and facts. Character and conduct are involved as well as words. A person can tell the truth in such a way as to deceive. Or, he can say something that is true, but by withholding part of the truth, communicate error. In other words, truth may be manipulated by untrue persons to achieve their own ends.

Take, for example, the simple statement: "Science has not proved the existence of God." This is a true statement. Science has not proved the existence of God because its methods are not capable of probing spiritual reality. Science deals with physical, measurable things because that is all its methods can handle.

Now suppose a person is arguing against the existence of God and says: "Science has not proved the existence of God"; leaving the impression that the scientific method is capable of proving the existence of God and it has tried and failed. The true words plus the false impression may lead people to believe that science has proved there is no God. In other words, the true statement, "Science has not proved the existence of God," has been so handled as to communicate the error, "Science has proved there is no God."

Now God wants everyone to be the kind of person who speaks the truth for true reasons. In other words, truth is a way of life for him. To illustrate, a storekeeper left his clerk in charge of the store while he went on an errand. A customer came in and asked the clerk to do something dishonest, remarking that he could do it because his master was out. "You are mistaken, sir," said the clerk. "My Master is Jesus Christ, and He is never out."

Significantly, when Jesus said, "I am . . . the truth" (John 14:6), He also said, "I am the way . . . and the life." The truth is a way of life. As Professor Horne says in *The Philosophy of Christian Education* (NY: Fleming H. Revell Co., 1937): "Truth to Jesus was primarily something to be done, not to be known. It is the right life, not the quality of correctness inherent in a proposition."

Liberating Truth

How does one become a truthful person? He

must enter into the living way of truth by accepting Jesus as Saviour. Until he accepts Christ, he is a child of the devil. Of Satan, Jesus said: "He was a murderer from the beginning, and abode not in the truth, because there is no truth in him. When he speaketh a lie, he speaketh of his own: for he is a liar, and the father of it" (John 8:44).

Those who accept Christ as Saviour and Lord are liberated from the guilt and bondage of sin. Christ is the Truth who sets men free. Other truth may dispel ignorance and superstition, but only Christ can set sinners free from their bondage.

Men will offer all kinds of excuses to avoid accepting Christ and freedom from sin's guilt and power. Satan makes it easy for them to delude themselves. (Read 2 Corinthians 4:4.) Satan keeps men in spiritual ignorance by keeping them convinced that spiritual error is truth, and that spiritual truth is error. He makes them keep on believing that their views are "reasonable," "intelligent," "common sense," or "scientific." Actually, their views are none of these. They are merely excuses they offer to avoid facing their foolishness and utter folly in saying, "There is no God" (Psalm 14:1).

There is a much better approach to life than this. One can be set free indeed through Him who is Truth indeed! Then with Paul he can exclaim: "The law of the Spirit of life in Christ Jesus hath made me free from the law of sin and death" (Romans 8:2).